SCREEN ADAPTATIONS
JANE AUSTEN'S
PRIDE AND PREJUDICE
THE RELATIONSHIP BETWEEN TEXT AND FILM

DEBORAH CARTMELL

methuen | drama

Methuen Drama

1 3 5 7 9 10 8 6 4 2

First published in 2010

Methuen Drama
A & C Black Publishers Ltd
36 Soho Square
London W1D 3QY
www.methuendrama.com

A CIP catalogue record for this book is available from the British Library

ISBN: 978 1 408 10593 1

Typeset by Margaret Brain, Wisbech, Cambs
Printed and bound in Great Britain by CPI Cox & Wyman,
Reading, Berkshire

contents

···

Part Three: Critical responses and the afterlife of the novel's adaptations

acknowledgements

I am extremely grateful to the British Academy and the Leverhulme Trust for enabling much of this research and to De Montfort University, in particular Philip Cox, for providing me with time to work at both the British Library and the British Film Institute. I've benefitted from the advice and encouragement of a number of individuals, in particular Imelda Whelehan, Jake Bradley and Hester Bradley, for their insights and comments. I've been lucky enough to share some of this work with my students whose visual literacy never fails to astonish me and I'm grateful to both Jonathan Powell and Andrew Davies for their time. Thanks to Ian Bradley and Imelda Whelehan for reading a draft and saving me from more than one embarrassing error (including 'Bryon' for 'Byron') and finally, thanks go to Jenny Ridout at Methuen Drama for her continued support and patience.

All passages from *Pride and Prejudice* are taken from the 1966 edition, ed. Donald Gray, reprinted 2001, published by W.W. Norton, New York and London.

PART 1:
Literary contexts

'Before the picture in earnest contemplation': a timeline of *pride and prejudice* adaptations

The time has come when a work on an adaptation of a literary text need not open with an apology, in response to accusations of 'dumbing down' or to those in Literary and Film Studies who have historically banned literary adaptations from admittance into their respective fields.[1] And, certainly, the time is ripe for a full length study of one of the most adapted of all novels, Jane Austen's *Pride and Prejudice*; and in Jane Austen's words, we come 'before the picture in earnest contemplation'.

In spite of a lack of sustained scholarly attention, filmed novels and plays have always generated heated debates. Adaptations of literary works have been around since the beginning of cinema: among the many earliest adaptations were versions of *Hansel and Gretel* (1897), *Cinderella* (1898, 1899), *Alladin and the Wonderful Lamp* (1900), *Cyrano de Bergerac* (1900), *Alice in Wonderland* (1903), *A Christmas Carol* (1910), and *Romeo and Juliet* (1900).

[1] For an account of the exclusion of film adaptations of literary texts from both English and Film Studies, see Deborah Cartmell and Imelda Whelehan, *Screen Adaptation: Impure Cinema* (Houndmills: Palgrave, 2010).

Conspicuous for her absence from early cinema is Jane Austen. While filmmakers in the silent period produced plenty of adaptations of the plays of Shakespeare and the novels of Dickens, Charlotte Brontë, and Tolstoy, it seems that no cinematic value or potential was detected in Austen's novels.

It's easy to understand why: stripped of their words, the novels would appear quite absurd; while Shakespeare's narratives normally have a sweeping grand scale (hence the many early adaptations of his works), nothing much happens in Austen's stories, the pleasure being in the choice of words and in the verbal subtleties. Even Austen's 19th century readers were struck by the lack of action as Margaret Oliphant summarises in her essay in *Blackwood's* (1870): 'The neglect which leaves the delicate heroine without a horse to ride, or the injury conveyed in the fact that she has to travel post without a servant, is the worst that happens.'[2] For a cinema that was deemed in the early period, 'the art form of democracy', Austen's restricted subject matter, not to mention class representation, would not be appropriate material.

As far as *Pride and Prejudice* goes, it's hard to imagine a silent version. Elizabeth's mortification upon overhearing Darcy's initial rejection of her at the Assembly ball would be difficult to render without words. How could a verbal rebuke be translated into a purely visual medium other than to have Darcy plugging his nose and pointing at Elizabeth in disgust? Darcy's letter would have to be shown with Elizabeth reading accompanied by an interminable number of flashbacks. It's not surprising that Austen waited until the sound era, especially given the frequency of radio dramatisations, to make her film debut. There have been several stage adap-

---

[2] 'Miss Austen and Miss Mitford', *Blackwood's* 107 (1870), pp. 294–6, reprinted in *Pride and Prejudice*, ed. Donald Gray (1966; 3rd ed. New York: Norton, 2001), p. 291.

tations, including a version by A.A. Milne entitled *Miss Elizabeth Bennet* (1936) and a Broadway musical, *First Impressions* (1959). The first recorded filming is a television adaptation of *Pride and Prejudice* in 1938 (in fact, the first recorded filming of an Austen novel) and, since then, the novel has found a home in television on many occasions, whereas there have only been two major 'faithful' film versions of the novel, the 1940 film starring Laurence Olivier and Greer Garson and the 2005 film with Keira Knightly and Matthew McFadden. Excluding spin-offs or loose adaptations (like *Bride and Prejudice*, 2004, and *Bridget Jones's Diary*, 2001), there are two films and seven television adaptations, ranging from 1938 to 1995, reflecting the highly 'adaptagenic' nature of the novel in the sound era.

This section surveys the various *Pride and Prejudice* adaptations from 1938 to the early 21st century and those features of the novel that have become identified with what has become known as the 'classic adaptation'. While the novel is seen as eminently adapt-able, Austen's text poses a number of problems for adaptation, problems that are also considered in this section. The critical reception of the novel in the 19th and 20th centuries and the novel's place within both canonical and popular traditions is considered in 'The novel and its reputation' (pp. 25–45). The book on screen is the subject of the following four sections in which *Pride and Prejudice* adaptations are separated into television, film, 'loose', and autobiographical readings. The final section ('Critical responses and the afterlife of the novel' (pp. 125–136)) considers the extensive 'afterlife' of the novel, especially in its 'paratexts', including internet sites, games, dolls, and the effects of earlier and later performances of the actors who have taken parts in the adaptations, who sometimes unwittingly carry the baggage of *Pride and Prejudice* into other roles.

A chronological list of *Pride and Prejudice* adaptations is difficult, if not impossible to compile, and the following consists of the most obvious – or 'straightforward' screen versions of the novel.

1938 Pride and Prejudice (UK), BBC

Unfortunately, typical of this vintage of broadcast, there appear to be no surviving recordings of this production. Archiving broadcasts is a relatively recent enterprise, the storage of kinescope and video recordings was implemented in hindsight in the 1970s but tended to be selective and hit and miss. Given that the 1938 *Pride and Prejudice* was transmitted from Alexandra Palace with a guaranteed range of a mere 25 miles, it's not surprising that it didn't make a long-lasting impact. However, from 1940, adaptations of Jane Austen's first novel on screen emerge with noticeable regularity.

1940 Pride and Prejudice (US), directed by Robert Z. Leonard, Metro-Goldwyn-Mayer

Starring Greer Garson as Elizabeth and Laurence Olivier as Darcy, this MGM film is in the tradition of the 'Screwball Comedy' of the 1930s and 40s. Sue Parrill describes Garson as 'too old and too knowing for this role'[3] and Darcy's superciliousness as heavy handed. Adapted by Jane Murfin and Aldous Huxley, based on the dramatisation by Helen Jerome, this is a much pared-down version of the story. Notable changes include Mr Collins as a librarian rather than a vicar (so as not to bring offence to the clergy), the Assembly ball and the ball at Netherfield compressed into one Assembly ball (in which Elizabeth behaves with uncharacteristic rudeness, refusing to dance with Darcy and seconds later accepting a dance with Wickham), the excision of

[3] Sue Parrill, *Jane Austen on Film and Television: A Critical Study of the Adaptations* (Jefferson, North Carolina, and London: McFarland, 2002), p. 52.

the visit to Pemberley, and the transformation of Lady Catherine into a kindly old lady, her visit to Elizabeth designed as a test to determine that Elizabeth is attracted to Darcy for love rather than money.

1949 Pride and Prejudice *(US), directed by Fred Coe, NBC (The Philco Television Playhouse)*

This version of the novel appeared live in black and white on NBC's Philco Television Playhouse on the 23 January 1949, sandwiched between adaptations, such as *A Christmas Carol, Cyrano de Bergerac* and *Twelfth Night*, and starred Madge Evans as Elizabeth and John Baragrey as Darcy. Omitting Charlotte Lucas, Mr Collins, Lady Catherine de Bourgh, Mary and Kitty Bennet, Mrs Philips, Georgiana Darcy, Colonel Fitzwilliam, the Forsters, and Captain Denny, this series adds Jane Austen to supplement the story.

1952 Pride and Prejudice *(UK), directed by Campbell Logan, BBC*

First broadcast on 2 February 1952, this is the first television mini-series of the novel, consisting of six episodes, starring Daphne Slater as Elizabeth and Peter Cushing as Darcy. Jane Austen, herself, is portrayed in all six episodes.

1958 Pride and Prejudice *(UK), produced by Barbara Burnham, BBC*

As a reflection of its popularity, the novel returns to television six years after the first mini-series with Jane Downs and Alan Badel in the leading roles. According to fans who watched this at the time of its broadcast, Badel is remembered as a definitive Darcy.

1967 **Pride and Prejudice** *(UK), directed by Joan Craft, BBC*

This series, again broadcast in six episodes, stars Celia Bannerman and Lewis Fiander, scripted by Nemone Lethbridge. Rather than filmed theatre, this adaptation used location shooting, including scenes set in Bath, Lacock Village and Dryham Park in Wiltshire. Its popularity is evident in the fact that it was re-broadcast in 1969. This adaptation omits Mary.

1980 **Pride and Prejudice** *(UK), directed by Cyril Coke, BBC*

Feminist novelist Fay Weldon produced the screenplay for this adaptation in five parts, starring Elizabeth Garvie and David Rintoul. The first episode was broadcast on the 13 January 1980, and for many this remains the best ever, according to the user reviews on the Internet Movie Database: 'In a few places, the pace is stilted, and it was clearly made for TV before big budgets, fancy sets, and more modern technology. Nevertheless, if someone wants to view an adaptation true to Austen's creation, this is an enjoyable experience.'[4]

1995 **Pride and Prejudice** *(UK), directed by Simon Langton, BBC*

Without doubt this six-part mini-series is the most successful adaptation to date, largely down to Colin Firth's Darcy, and Andrew Davies' script that draws out the male figures in what has always been regarded as a female-centred story. Unlike Elizabeth Garvie's restrained high-necked dresses, Jennifer Ehle's Elizabeth is almost always seen with plunging necklines, contributing to the rewriting of the novel in a thickly veiled sex-romp format. The production was a

---

[4] http://www.imdb.com/title/tt0078672/usercomments?start=0. Accessed 6/01/10

huge success, producing a new phenomenon named by the press as 'Darcymania', largely due to the much commented on plunge Darcy takes in the lake at Pemberley. As Andrew Davies has wryly observed, in spite of being a popular novelist and screenwriter for numerous productions, he'll probably be best remembered for putting Mr Darcy in a wet shirt.[5]

2003 Pride and Prejudice: A Latter Day Comedy (US), directed by Andrew Black, Excel Entertainment

According to everyone I've spoken to who has had the misfortune to see this film, the less said about this 'adaptation', the better, and it's not surprising that it's not managed to attract any critical attention, as a second viewing would be unthinkable for most viewers. In this version, set in Mormon Utah, Elizabeth is a very diligent college student, unwilling to think of boyfriends until she graduates. And then along comes playboy Wickham and business-man Darcy, in a very badly acted and transparently low budget production. While the novel, it seems, should lend itself to a teenpic version (as demonstrated so successfully by the adaptation of *Emma* in *Clueless*, 1995), to date, surprisingly, *Pride and Prejudice* has been unable to break into this genre on the big screen. The film sunk into oblivion indecently quickly and as *The Lost Angeles Times* review observes, it was disappointing on every level: 'anyone familiar with the book or BBC mini-series (or over the age of six) will not be surprised by the outcome, except for how wholly unengaging and tedious it is made here'.[6] As Steve Rhodes observes: 'When a filmmaker can't find an original story idea, the

[5] Andrew Davies in conversation (unpublished), De Montfort University, July 2003.
[6] Kevin Crust, 30 April 2004, http://www.calendarlive.com/movies/reviews/cl-et-pride30apr30,2,340437.story. Accessed 22/03/10.

temptation is to fall back on a classic, say Jane Austen's "Pride and Prejudice". Director Andrew Black probably thought how wrong could he go with that? With a script that reimagines the story as happening with today's twenty somethings, surely the tale will speak to modern audiences, he must have reasoned. Well, this ineptly directed and lamely scripted – by Anne K. Black, Jason Faller and Katherine Swigert – PRIDE AND PREJUDICE falls as flat on its face as a teenage girl trying on her first pair of high heels. It's a moderately Mormon movie that has just enough church references to place the film in the Mormon movie genre, but it's one of the worst examples of a surprisingly rich and frequently successful group of pictures.'[7]

While some reviewers conclude that the film is proof that *Pride and Prejudice* cannot be adapted to a contemporary setting, most agree that this is just a very poor quality adaptation, easily forgotten and unworthy of critical commentary.

2004 Bride and Prejudice *(UK), directed by Gurinder Chadha, Pathé Pictures International*

This Bollywood-style adaptation, directed by Gurinder Chadha, demonstrates the ease with which Austen's novel can be translated into a different cultural context. Starring former Miss World and leading Bollywood actress, Aishwarya Rai, the majority of the film's setting is in Amritsar, India, where Lalita (the Elizabeth character) meets, dislikes, and finally marries the American, William Darcy, played by Martin Henderson. Racial or cultural differences don't seem to be at the heart of the couple's antagonism, but the breathtakingly beautiful shots of Amritsar completely upstage the scenes in London and California, visually suggesting that it is Darcy

[7] http://www.imdb.com/Reviews/377/37723. Accessed 22/03/10.

not Elizabeth who converts to a new set of priorities. His attraction is as much to the place as it is to the person living there.

2005 Pride & Prejudice *(UK, France), directed by Joe Wright, Focus Features, Universal, Working Title Films*

As in the 1940 film starring Greer Garson and Laurence Olivier, the second major film feature uses celebrity status in the form of Keira Knightley as Elizabeth, and, to a lesser extent, Judi Dench as Lady Catherine, to draw in the crowds. Directed by Joe Wright with a screenplay by Deborah Moggach, the film clearly tries to distinguish itself from the popular 1995 adaptation by setting the story in the late 18th rather than the early 19th century, when the novel was first drafted. The emphasis here is on the relative poverty of the Bennets, in contrast to the 1995 adaptation, the screenwriter Deborah Moggach coining it 'the muddy hem version'.[8]

2007 Becoming Jane *(UK, USA), directed by Julian Jarrold, Ecosse Films, BBC Films*

In line with a tendency in *Pride and Prejudice* adaptations to read Elizabeth Bennet as a version of Jane Austen herself (as will be discussed in '*Pride and Prejudice* as concealed autobiography' pp. 109–122), this film, directed by Julian Jarrold, based on the biography by Jon Spence, *Becoming Jane Austen*, 2003, recreates Jane Austen as a replica of Elizabeth Bennet (with a touch of the impetuous Lydia thrown in). Starring Anne Hathaway and James McAvoy, like its predecessors, the film draws on famous actors, in particular Julie Walters and Maggie Smith (so often included in 'heritage' films) to draw a large audience. The following year saw

[8] Deborah Moggach, 3rd Annual Association of Adaptation Studies Conference, Amsterdam, 25/09/08.

the television biography, *Miss Austen Regrets* in which a much older Austen, played by Olivia Williams, becomes a version of *Persuasion's* Anne Elliott.

The above list is by necessity selective and the sheer volume of adaptations – what Gérard Genette identifies as 'hypertexts' in his account of transtextuality[9] – is testimony to the canonical status of Austen's novel, but it's worth noting that it's not until the mid 20th century that Austen adaptations become regular events in film and television schedules. It's fair to say that since the beginning of the television era, there's been a *Pride and Prejudice* for every generation, providing us with an opportunity to chart how the book has changed in its various readings. Conclusions to be drawn from the above list are that *Pride and Prejudice* has increased in status from the last half of the 20th century, it has been deemed more appropriate to television than to film and that film adaptations don't really get going until the 21st century.

The episodic nature of her writing and the variety of subplots seem to be more at home in television than in film. While film is character-driven, normally focussing on two central characters, Austen's novels involve a large variety of characters whose relationships are complexly understated and require the time to unfold that only television allows. As Suzanne R. Pucci and James Thompson observe, 'the Austen Phenomenon' is at its heart concerned with makeovers, a subject which Austen covertly introduces us to in *Emma* in the heroine's makeover of her new

---

[9] See Robert Stam, 'Introduction: The Theory and Practice of Adaptation', *Literature and Film: A Guide to the Theory and Practice of Adaptation*, ed. Robert Stam and Alessandra Raengo (Malden and Oxford: Blackwell, 2005) pp. 26–31 for an application of Genette's 'transtextuality' to adaptations.

friend, Harriet Smith.[10] *Pride and Prejudice* has been made over into a range of productions, from Bollywood to teenpic, from heritage cinema to romantic comedy. This study is largely confined to those adaptations that position themselves as adaptations or conform to the 'genre' of adaptation, as outlined by Thomas Leitch in his essay, 'Adaptation: the Genre'[11] and emerging from what film director François Truffaut calls, in a derogatory sense, the 'Tradition of Quality' in which films (needlessly, for Truffaut) seek respectability from their literary sources.[12] For Leitch, to qualify as an adaptation *qua* adaptation, a film must call attention to written texts and period detail, featuring period setting, period music, lay an emphasis on words and writing, and make use of intertitles. I would also add that the adaptation should be of a canonical text, emphasising what it perceives as its cultural worth through the incorporation of works of art (painting, sculpture, architecture) while paying implicit or explicit tributes to its author. And as the majority of audiences for this sort of film are female, the films tend to pander to a female audience by adding female-friendly episodes to the storyline. In *Pride and Prejudice* adaptations these have taken the form of Elizabeth triumphing over Darcy at a game of archery (1940), Jane showing off her cricket skills in *Becoming Jane* (2007) and, most obviously, Darcy stripping off and jumping into a pond in Andrew Davies' adaptation of 1995, creating

[10] 'The Jane Austen Phenomenon: Remaking the Past at the Millennium', *Jane Austen and Co.: Remaking the Past in Contemporary Culture*, eds Suzanne R. Pucci and James Thompson (New York: State University of New York Press, 2003), pp.1–12.

[11] Thomas Leitch, 'Adaptation, the Genre', *Adaptation*, 1(2), 2008, pp. 106–120.

[12] 'A Certain Tendency of the French Cinema' (1966) in *The Film Studies Reader*, eds Joanne Hollows, Peter Hutchings and Mark Jancovich (London: Arnold, 2000), pp. 58–62.

sensational viewing for the female audience. Another feature of such a genre, as Christine Geraghty has persuasively argued, is an emphasis on the film's status as an adaptation (i.e. a mechanical reproduction) through references to new technologies and new forms of communication.[13]

While, as Geraghty illustrates, in an adaptation such as *Atonement* (2007), the emphasis is on the typewriter, in Austen's novels, 'new technology' and meta-narrative episodes are present, I suggest, in the entertainment afforded by the playing of the pianoforte. Annette Davison writes about the significance of the instrument in the novels, a significance that is also translated to screen:

> In the late eighteenth century, possession of a piano demonstrated wealth and position. Innovations in the development of the instrument offered social opportunities that earlier keyboard instruments, such as the spinet and the clavichord, could not furnish; the hammer action of the pianoforte enabled the production of a much greater dynamic range . . . In a period well before radios or gramophone players, when professional concerts in England were held generally only in London or Bath, amateur music-making offered opportunities for young people not available elsewhere: in particular, legitimated (i.e. chaperoned) contact with members of the opposite sex.[14]

The playing of the instrument in the novel, the must-have and most up-to-date form of entertainment, provides an opportunity to

[13] Christine Geraghty, 'Foregrounding of Media in *Atonement*', *Adaptation* 2 (2), 2009, pp. 91–109.

[14] Annette Davison, 'High Fidelity? Music in Screen Adaptations', *The Cambridge Companion to Literature on Screen*, eds Deborah Cartmell and Imelda Whelehan (Cambridge: Cambridge University Press, 2007), p. 215.

combine consumerism and eroticism and a model for erotic shorthand in 'heritage' cinema, such as the Merchant Ivory production of *A Room with a View* (1986) and climaxing in Jane Campion's *The Piano* (1993). Even though the latter film is not an adaptation, its use of features we associate with adaptations, especially the fetishisation of the piano, in what Ken Gelder has identified as 'literary cinema',[15] gives it an honorary status as such.

Austen's narratives are replete with such moments, affording her adapters numerous occasions to call attention to their own works' status as adaptations. Frank Churchill's present of the pianoforte to Jane Fairfax in *Emma* arouses irrepressible speculation, involving coded conjectures about the meaning of the instrument.

> She did not wish to speak of the pianoforte, she felt too much in the secret herself, to think the appearance of curiosity or interest fair, and therefore purposely kept at a distance: but by the others, the subject was almost immediately introduced and she saw the blush of consciousness with which congratulations were received, the blush of guilt which accompanied the name of 'my excellent friend, Col. Campbell'.[16]

Mary's aborted piano playing at Netherfield, signalling her sexual unattractiveness and disqualification from the marriage market, is mirrored later in the novel by Lady Catherine's unsuccessful attempt to relegate Elizabeth's displays of passion (or piano playing) to Mrs Jenkinson's (translated in most adaptations as the housekeeper's) quarters, a place where she would be safely

[15] Ken Gelder, 'Jane Campion and the Limits of Literary Cinema', *Adaptations: From Text to Screen, Screen to Text*, eds Deborah Cartmell and Imelda Whelehan (London: Routledge, 1999), pp. 157–71.

[16] Jane Austen, *Emma* (Harmondsworth: Penguin, 1994), p.166.

removed from the male gaze. Charlotte Lucas, possessor of the cynically realistic view of courtship, enigmatically asks Elizabeth to play at Lucas Lodge with the rhetorical statement: 'I am going to open the instrument, Eliza, and you know what follows' (17). Striking in these novels, is the seemingly gratuitous praise or interest lavished upon the instrument. The reiteration of how well Elizabeth plays in *Pride and Prejudice* calls attention to the uncertainty of Elizabeth's performances: she claims she plays badly, while Darcy's response to her playing implies the opposite.[17] The association of a musical instrument with both spiritual and physical intercourse has its roots as early as Shakespeare:

> How oft, when thou, my music, music play'st,
> Upon that blessèd wood whose motion sounds
> With thy sweet fingers when thou gently sway'st
> The wiry concord that mine ear confounds,
> Do I envy those jacks that nimble leap,
> To kiss the tender inward of thy hand
> Whilst my poor lips, which should that harvest reap,
> At the wood's boldness by thee blushing stand!
> To be so tickled, they would change their state
> And situation with those dancing chips,
> O'er whom thy fingers walk with gentle gait,
> Making dead wood more blessed than living lips.
>   Since saucy jacks so happy are in this,
>   Give them thy fingers, me thy lips to kiss. (128)[18]

[17] For a discussion of the Carl Davis score for the 1995 adaptation, see Davison, pp. 212–225.

[18] Sonnet 128, *The Oxford Shakespeare: The Complete Works*, 2nd ed., eds John Jowett, William Montgomery, Gary Taylor and Stanley Wells (Oxford: Oxford University Press, 2005).

Compare Shakespeare's analogy between playing the virginals and sexual intercourse with the parallel Elizabeth draws between playing and social intercourse:

> 'My fingers,' said Elizabeth, 'do not move over this instrument in the masterly manner which I see so many women's do. They have not the same force or rapidity, and do not produce the same expression. But then I have always supposed it to be my own fault – because I would not take the trouble of practising. It is not that I do not believe *my* fingers as capable as any other woman's of superior execution.'
>
> Darcy smiled and said, 'You are perfectly right. You have employed your time much better. No one admitted to the privilege of hearing you, can think any thing wanting. We neither of us perform to strangers.' (116–117)

The salivation over the pianoforte in the novels is significantly, and perhaps increasingly, pronounced in the adaptations, calling attention to themselves as classic adaptations par excellence. Austen's novels, especially in their unashamed relishing over the new technologies of the day, in the shape of the pianoforte, provide adapters with a model for a specific and instantly recognisable type of classic adaptation. Coincidentally, perhaps, the scene in which Elizabeth plays the piano at Pemberley, with an enamoured Darcy looking on, is Andrew Davies' declared favourite moment in his 1995 series.[19]

In an interview published in 2007, Andrew Davies (adapter of the 1995 television adaptation) claims that Jane Austen is the easiest of

---

[19] 'A practical understanding of literature on screen: two conversations with Andrew Davies, interviewed by Deborah Cartmell and Imelda Whelehan, *The Cambridge Companion to Literature on Screen*, pp. 239–251.

all writers to adapt because she is so precise in every detail, but also because she has contributed so much to the genre of romantic comedy through the structures of her novels. The precision in detail means that viewers don't concern themselves with discontinuity or implausibility as they may, for instance with an adaptation of *Wuthering Heights*. Visualising the novel leads adapters and viewers with a number of questions, somehow more pertinent to screen than to fiction where we are more inclined to suspend disbelief. With the exception of why Lady Catherine travels all the way to Longbourn when she could have written a letter or sent a henchman, *Pride and Prejudice* leaves adapters with no puzzles to solve or loose ends to tie up. *Wuthering Heights* adaptations, on the other hand, provoke an array of questions in the translation to screen, such as why did Mr Earnshaw walk to Liverpool when he clearly has horses (given he buys a crop as a present for Cathy) and how could he have carried a boy on his shoulders all that way? Dickens, similarly, dismays film adapters with numerous loose ends, such as what happens to Mr Guppy in *Bleak House*, or what becomes of Miss Wade, in *Little Dorrit*; their stories are left frustratingly untold when they cease to be of use to the main narrative. Austen's accessibility to cinema is also astutely noted by George Bluestone in the first book length study devoted to the topic of literature on screen (1957), commenting that *Pride and Prejudice*, 'given the special attributes of its style, possesses the essential ingredients of a movie script'.[20] Sarah Cardwell observes that 'Austen adaptations had by the 1990s become representative of the genre of classic-novel adaptations as a whole' and have 'played a vital role in consolidating the traits which adaptations

---

[20] George Bluestone, *Novels into Film: The Metamorphosis of Fiction into Cinema* (Berkeley: University of California Press, 1957), p. 117.

share (and which make them all "look the same")'.[21] David Monaghan, in the introduction to *The Cinematic Jane Austen: Essays on the Filmic Sensibility of the Novels* (co-written with Ariane Hudelet and John Wiltshire, 2009) makes a similar case for the filmic quality of Austen's fictions with regard to 'the archetypal or universal nature of her basic plot and character functions';[22] in particular, these attributes lay the groundwork for the romantic comedy. At the centre of such a genre are *Pride and Prejudice* adaptations. Indeed Austen's novel provides the template for so many romantic comedies as well as repeatedly being repackaged into 'heritage productions'. Its fairytale qualities and its 'shamelessly wish fulfilling qualities'[23] seem at odds with its more serious dimensions, but nonetheless explain why the narrative structure is so frequently used in romantic comedies.

Both Bluestone and Davies recognise in Austen and, more particularly *Pride and Prejudice*, the 'template' for the archetypal adaptation, the recognisable features for which I argue to be: an emphasis on words (the reading of letters in the novel), references to art (the portrait gallery in Pemberley and the houses in the novel themselves), female friendly episodes (Elizabeth's upstaging Darcy in verbal sparring), and an emphasis on new technologies via the pianoforte episodes. The 'adaptation genre' also involves 'historical music' and requires the source to be canonical. And, of course

21 Sarah Cardwell, *Adaptation Revisited: Television and the Classic Novel* (Manchester: Manchester University Press, 2002), p. 134.

22 David Monaghan, 'Introduction', *The Cinematic Jane Austen: Essays on the Filmic Sensibility of the Novels*, David Monaghan, Ariane Hudelet and John Wiltshire (Jefferson, North Carolina: McFarlane, 2009), p. 15.

23 Claudia L. Johnson, '*Pride and Prejudice* and the Pursuit of Happiness', in *Jane Austen and the Discourses of Feminism*, ed. Devoney Looser (New York: St Martin's Press, 1995), p. 348.

Austen is second only to Shakespeare as a canonical author. Almost parroting Shakespeare adaptations, Austen's fictions have been subjected to popular translations involving time travelling (Dr Who's *The Shakespeare Code*, 2007, and *Lost in Austen*, 2009) and autobiographical readings of the texts (*Romeo and Juliet* becomes *Shakespeare in Love*, 1998, and *Pride and Prejudice* is translated into *Becoming Jane*, 2007).

The number and range of *Pride and Prejudice* adaptations invite a variety of approaches. Julie Sanders distinguishes adaptations from appropriations insofar as the source text in the latter is only of incidental importance: 'appropriation frequently affects a more decisive journey away from the informing source into a wholly new cultural product and domain.'[24] Nonetheless, what can be regarded as 'straight' adaptations of the novel invariably rewrite the story for a particular audience, so that Fay Weldon's script of 1980 focuses on the women, almost valorising Mrs Bennet whose objection to the entailing of the estate in preference for the male line is seen to have considerable justification. Andrew Davies, in what has been identified as a post-feminist age, uniquely gives voice to the men, especially, of course Mr Darcy, who is seen where he isn't in the novel, to be undergoing an almost Herculean effort to suppress his powerful feelings for Elizabeth.

If we take a narratological approach, as recommended by Brian McFarlane in *Novel to Film*, adaptations can be unpacked not by what is left out (the unprofitable, 'not as good as the book' line of argument), but what is added, such as visual, linguistic or cinematic codes. McFarlane notes that a film adds to the cardinal functions of a novel (which may or may not be retained by a film), a new set of codes, such as:

[24] Julie Sanders, *Adaptation and Appropriation* (Abingdon and New York: Routledge, 2006), p. 26.

- Cinematic codes: for example 'fade out' signals to the audience that a flashback is about to occur
- Language codes: accents and voice tones
- Visual codes: what is selected or interpreted visually
- Non-linguistic codes: music and other aural codes
- Cultural codes: the depiction of the way people live, time and places.[25]

The erasure of all the other dancers in the ball at Netherfield, in the 2005 adaptation, leaves Darcy and Elizabeth literally dancing on their own; it is a cinematic code, signalling to the audience that this is *their* story and, unbeknown to them while clear to their audience, they only have eyes for each other. A particularly memorable occurance of this cinematic device is in *West Side Story* (1961), in which a dissolve erases everyone around the central couple on the dance floor, visually announcing that the two are 'made for each other'.

Intertextuality is another approach to adaptations which relegates the source text to just one of numerous references to other texts. Jane's dumbfounding of the hero in her triumph at cricket, in *Becoming Jane*, for instance, can be read as an intertextual refence to Elizabeth's triumph over Darcy in archery in the 1940s *Pride and Prejudice* and/or Emma's victory in archery in the 1996 adaptation, directed by Douglas McGrath. Another attempt to rescue the study of adaptation from the fidelity model (in which all that can be said is that the film can't be truly faithful to the novel or hypotext, and ergo, must be inferior) is to create taxonomies of adaptations (although these can be argued to covertly position different types of adaptations in relation to their

---

[25] Brian McFarlane, *Novel to Film: An Introduction to the Theory of Adaptation* (Oxford: Oxford University Press, 1996), pp. 28–29.

proximity and therefore their fidelity to the novel).[26] For instance, an adaptation may seek to 'preserve' the novel, or it may aim to impose a particular interpretation on its hypotext or it may seek to translate it entirely, creating a new text which may aim to confront or indeed rival the 'original'. However, classification causes as many problems as it solves. Andrew Davies' acclaimed BBC adaptation has been regarded as a 'preservation' of Austen's text in its attention to language and historical detail, an 'interpretation' as it rereads the novel from a male rather than female perspective, and as a 'translation' as it is inevitably of its own time rather than a recreation of the early 19th century. Nonetheless, these categories are of use in ordering the bewildering array of screen *Pride and Prejudice*s: the television adaptations which endeavour to offer the viewer the closest approximation to *reading* the novel (and to inspire subsequent reading), the film adaptations which interpret the novel as a reflection on the present as much as the past (such as the 1940 *Pride and Prejudice* in its portrayal of an Edenic England, worthy of fighting for on the brink of the American engagement with the Second World War), and in the looser adaptations, in which the novel's structure is re-embellished to fit a particular reading, whether it be biographical or in a contemporary refashioning (from *Becoming Jane* to *Lost in Austen*).

Essentially, this book takes a chronological perspective on the many *Pride and Prejudice*s, regarding adaptations as appropriations, inspired by the New Historicist and Cultural Materialist

[26] Early examples of taxonomies of adaptation can be found in Jack Jorgens' three types of adaptation in his analysis of Olivier's *Henry V*: theatrical, realist, and filmic (*Shakespeare on Film*, Bloomington and London: Indiana University Press, 1977). Geoffrey Wagner also posits three types of adaptation: transposition, commentary, and analogy. *The Novel and the Cinema* (Rutherford, New Jersey: Fairleigh Dickinson University Press, 1989).

approaches of the early 1980s. For most of us, the process and study of adaptation so often begins with the intention succinctly summarised by Stephen Greenblatt in his famous pronouncement in *Shakespearean Negotiations*: 'I began with a desire to speak with the dead' and ends, as in Greenblatt's own historical questing, with the realisation that 'all I could hear was my own voice'.[27] Adaptations are akin to what Paul Hamilton identifies as 'criticism' that 'does not free us from the power it criticises, but recycles that power for its own purposes'.[28] An acknowledgement of the anachronistic quality present in all the screen versions of *Pride and Prejudice*, whether it is arguably incidental or accidental to the conception of an adaptation – for example the *Gone with the Wind*-inspired costumes of the 1940s film – or vital to its very conception – as in the mixture of the past with the present in *Lost in Austen*, a present which becomes the past the moment it's represented – is vital to our approach to adaptations, or what Suzanne R. Pucci and James Thompson identify as 'remakes' in their collect, *Jane Austen and Co: Remaking the Past in Contemporary Culture* (2003). For them, 'The past is made again – re-made as in a re-presentation – and yet the past is always made anew'. This remaking of the past is, like *Emma*'s transformation of Harriet Smith, a 'makeover': 'of shaping the past in the new fashions, styles, and desires of the present.'[29] Adaptations allow us to relish in and reflect upon the reciprocal relationship between the past and the present, and perhaps, even, between ourselves as readers of books and as viewers of films.

---

[27] Stephen Greenblatt, *Shakespearean Negotiations: The Circulation of Social Energy in Renaissance England* (Oxford: Clarendon Press, 1988), p.1.

[28] Paul Hamilton, *Historicism* (1996; 2nd ed. London: Routledge, 2003) p.140.

[29] Pucci and Thompson, p. 2.

Pride and Prejudice is a novel that owes much to the film and television industries for its unwavering popularity, but as I hope to demonstrate, the film and television industries owe at least as much to the novel for its contribution to the seemingly unstoppable genre of adaptation *qua* adaptation and to the enduring genre of romantic comedy, both of which appropriate the alleged escapism identified by readers of Austen's fiction.

'Honour, decorum, prudence': the novel and its reputation

The quality of Austen's writing is usefully summarised by Lady Catherine de Bourgh in her pronouncement on how Elizabeth ought to behave: with 'honour, decorum, prudence' and it has long been the norm to read Austen adaptations, accordingly, as attempts to preserve the *status quo*. And for many purists the alliance of Jane Austen's novels with cinema is, like Lady Catherine's view of the marriage of Elizabeth and Darcy, grossly incompatible given their different social positions.

A central problem encountered by all critics of adaptation studies is whether or not there is such a thing as an adaptation; it is a truth almost universally acknowledged that all texts are in one way or another, adaptations (and that all books on Jane Austen must somehow use that famous line). As Linda Hutcheon observes, an adaptation makes explicit the fact that all texts are based on other texts,[1] and this is certainly the case of the 'classic adaptation' as outlined in the previous section. How is literary influence to be distinguished from the 'source' text? The notion of a 'source text' is itself problematic, implying that an adaptation is a reworking of a single, given text with no other influences and that the source is, from beginning to end, 'original', having no literary or other

[1] Linda Hutcheon, *A Theory of Adaptation* (New York and London: Routledge, 2006).

influences. The idea of an 'original' is, of course, impossible. Every literary text builds upon what has gone before and is, by necessity, a product of its own environment. Even *Pride and Prejudice* has its 'sources' and can be viewed as a reworking of *Much Ado About Nothing* which, in turn, can be seen as a reworking of *The Taming of the Shrew*. Both plays, in many ways inversions of *Romeo and Juliet*'s love at first sight plot, begin with a man and a woman expressing detestation for each other and end with their marriage, a classic formula for Hollywood comedies. Austen's novel is within a long tradition of literary texts that explore the paradoxical closeness of the conditions of love and hate, from Shakespeare's dark lady sonnets or plays as diverse as *Much Ado About Nothing* and *Othello* to Middleton and Rowley's *The Changeling*. But in Austen's case, rather than the extremes of love and hate, the unsettling closeness is more between that of a tendency towards fondness and an inclination of some disaffection.

John Wiltshire explores Austen's reputation as the 'Prose Shakespeare' in *Recreating Jane Austen* (2001), recounting how Jane Austen has been given something like canonical equivalence to Shakespeare, while she is also regarded as an imitator of Shakespeare. For instance, Richard Simpson's important account in 1870 elevates Austen's status by drawing parallels between the novels and Shakespeare's plots and characters: 'Thus each of her characters, like Shakespeare's Richard II, "plays in one person many people", contains within him "a generation of still breeding thoughts", none of which is "self-contained" but all "intermixed", each modified by something else'.[2] Wiltshire reminds us that this

[2] Richard Simpson, *North British Review*, 1870, lii, pp. 129–52, *Jane Austen: The Critical Heritage 1811–1870*, vol. 1, ed. B.C. Southam (London: Routledge, 1979), p. 250.

view of Austen began immediately after publication of *Pride and Prejudice*, with the reviewer in *The Critical Reviewer* (March 1813) observing that Elizabeth Bennet 'takes great delight in playing *the Beatrice* upon 'Darcy'.[3] Certainly, Austen herself draws an implicit parallel between Darcy and Orsino in *Twelfth Night* in Darcy's observation to Elizabeth, referencing the opening of Shakespeare's play: 'I have been used to consider poetry as the *food* of love' (31). But as it's been suggested in the previous section, it really is *music* that is the food of love in *Pride and Prejudice*.

Up until the publication of *Pride and Prejudice* Austen had lived through the American Declaration of Independence (1776), the French Revolution (1789), the war with France (1793–1802) and the abolition of slavery (1807). The novels and especially *Pride and Prejudice*, known as the lightest of all Austen's fictions, are conspicuously quiet on anything to do with the political or social events of the time.

Nonetheless, the evolution of the novel from *First Impressions* (composed over 1796–97) to *Pride and Prejudice* (published in 1813) can be seen in the context of its representation of a society in flux, between 18th century pragmatism and the idealism of the 19th century. At the time Jane Austen was writing *Pride and Prejudice*, the country was experiencing the effects of the French Revolution whilst in the midst of the Napoleonic Wars. Jane Austen's cousin's husband had been beheaded in France and Austen herself had two brothers in the Royal Navy. Possibly due to the fact that, unlike Basil Fawlty, Austen studiously and successfully avoids

---

[3] John Wiltshire, *Recreating Jane Austen* (Cambridge: Cambridge University Press, 2001), p. 70. For another comparison of Shakespeare and Austen see Lisa Hopkins, *Relocating Shakespeare and Austen on Screen* (Houndmills: Palgrave, 2009).

explicit mention of war,[4] her novel has been popularly regarded as safe and apolitical, possibly inspired by Austen's own comments on her work in a letter to her sister, Cassandra:

> – Upon the whole however I am quite vain enough & well satisfied enough. – The work is rather too light & bright & sparkling; – it wants shade; – it wants to be stretched out here & there with a long Chapter – of sense if it could be had, if not of solemn nonsense – about something unconnected with the story; and Essay on Writing, a critique on Walter Scott, or the history of Buonaparte – or anything that would form a contrast & bring the reader with increased delight to the playfulness & Epigrammatism of the general stile.[5]

Austen's playful comments are an instance of both denial and affirmation, daring us (or Cassandra, at least) to look at the novel as an essay on poetics and politics, an approach readers, on the whole, have resisted. The view that the novel is simply 'bright & sparkling', wanting 'shade', has persisted. Although being credited with the responsibility of putting Austen on the academic map,[6]

[4] The only possible mention of the war is in Austen's closing remarks about Lydia and Wickham's restlessness after 'the restoration of peace' and as Isobel Armstrong notes, it is unclear whether this refers to 'the peace settled by the Treaty of Amiens (1802), or one of the much later pauses in the Peninsular War (possibly after the relief of Portugal, 1812), or a hypothetical peace.' 'Introduction', *Pride and Prejudice* (Oxford: Oxford University Press, 1990), pp. vii–xxvii, p. viii.

[5] 'To Cassandra Austen Saturday 6–Sunday 7 November 1814 Godmersham Park', reprinted in *Pride and Prejudice*, ed. Donald Gray (New York and London: Norton, 2001), pp. 274–5.

[6] See Deidre Lynch, 'Introduction: Sharing with our Neighbors', *Janeites: Austen's Disciples and Devotees*, ed. Deidre Lynch (Princeton and Oxford: Princeton University Press, 2000), p. 8.

D.W. Harding writing in *Scrutiny* in 1940 observes how she provided a refuge for those on their deathbeds, or for those who sought escape from the upheavals of the contemporary world.[7] Marilyn Butler notes that although *Pride and Prejudice* is regarded as 'the lightest, most consistently entertaining, and least didactic of the novels,'[8] the novel, according to her, is also a conservative attack on the contemporary doctrine of the faith in subjectivity. In spite of the tendency to regard the work as both escapist and narrow, Pat Rogers (2006) convincingly argues, the entire plot of the novel hinges on the movements of the militia, responding to the threat of a revolutionised France at the beginning of the Napoleonic Wars.[9] The shortage of men, the uncertainty regarding the future of Longbourn, the displacement of the oldest by the youngest (the mild mannered Jane for the unrestrained and thoughtless Lydia, as the first to marry), all reflect a larger society in a state of upheaval. As has been noted by many readers, the family structures within the novel are miniaturised social models and embedded in the text are discrete political and social debates, in particular, Austen quietly alerts us to injustices in distributions of property, often through the unlikely voice of Mrs Bennet ('I do think it is the hardest thing in the world, that your estate should be entailed away from your own children' (42)), the economic interpretation of marriage (epitomised by Mr Collins's uncontested definition of the object of matrimony to 'secure an amiable companion for the advantage of all (the) family' (78)), and the arbitrariness of class divisions (as when Darcy

[7] '"Regulated Hatred": An Aspect in the Work of Jane Austen', *Scrutiny* 8 (1940), pp. 351–54, reprinted in *Pride and Prejudice*, ed. Donald Gray, p. 296.

[8] Marilyn Butler, *Jane Austen and the War of Ideas* (Oxford: Clarendon Press, 1975), p. 197.

[9] Jane Austen, *Pride and Prejudice*, ed. Pat Rogers (Cambridge: Cambridge University Press, 2006), p. liv.

unexpectedly treats Elizabeth's aunt and uncle (who is 'in trade') with civility, she reflects: 'What will be his surprise . . . when he knows who they are! He takes them now for people of fashion' (165)).

Three major issues lurk beneath this seemingly harmless narrative surface: the constraints of patriarchy, the economics of marriage, and the injustices of class, divided in the novel between the aristocracy (Darcy and Lady Catherine), the gentry (the Bennet family) and 'trade' (the Gardiners). The novel can be divided into the events leading up to Elizabeth's three proposals. To a reader nowadays, Elizabeth's refusal of Mr Collins's proposal seems totally reasonable. However, considering her situation as a young woman with very little hope of making a match equal to her current status, it's perhaps not as 'reasonable' as it seems (and as Charlotte Lucas demonstrates). Nonetheless, Austen makes Elizabeth's choice obvious by relentlessly stripping the episode of any romantic association, making it an extreme case of pragmatism over romanticism. The family (and Elizabeth) know that she is Mr Collins's second choice (after Jane) and that the marriage has been planned even before Collins clapped eyes on any of the sisters in order, as Collins himself professes, to make 'atonement for inheriting their father's estate' and 'full of eligibility and suitableness, and excessively generous and disinterested on his own part' (48). The comedy emerges from Mr Collins's failure to comprehend or grasp that Elizabeth says 'no' to him at several times during the meeting. His three reasons for marrying are all to do with himself and rather than praise Elizabeth he manages to insert his uncontested belief that he is doing her the most generous of favours, inappropriately referring to the future 'melancholy event' of her father's death while insulting her by reminding her of her ultimate unworthiness ('it is by no means certain that another offer of marriage may ever be made you. Your portion is unhappily so small' (74)). While Mrs

Bennet is vehemently in favour of her daughter's marriage, Mr Bennet intervenes, refusing to allow it to go forward. In keeping with the patriarchal construction of the household, Mr Bennet has the final word: his argument is for the individual, Mrs Bennet's is for the greater good of society. In both of the 'couplings', Elizabeth and Collins, and Mr and Mrs Bennet, it is the men who come out as the most self-centred (Collins in the negative sense, Mr Bennet in the positive) while silencing the female point of view. The moral of the episode seems to be that women (i.e. Elizabeth) can and should speak out against men, but only with the sanction of patriarchy.

Mr Darcy's first proposal bears an uncanny similarity to that of Mr Collins, with Elizabeth in the same position of initially remaining silent with an unembellished 'no', followed by a more elaborate explanation for her refusal, but one that this time doesn't fall on deaf ears. Both Darcy and Collins preface their proposals with prescriptions for the ideal women. Darcy irritates Elizabeth with his portrait of the accomplished lady: to Miss Bingley's list of a 'thorough knowledge of music, singing, drawing, dancing and the modern languages' and 'a certain something in her air and manner of walking, the tone of her voice, her address and expressions', Darcy adds 'something more substantial, in the improvement of her mind by extensive reading' (27). This formula for an accomplished woman, something that could have been taken from a conduct book, is not a far remove from Mr Collins's reading to the Bennet family of another conduct book, Fordyce's *Sermons to Young Women* (1766), stopped at page three by an impatient Lydia. These high-minded pronouncements on how a woman should behave – for instance, 'Mental Acquisitions (are) of importance to your dignity and figure in life. Consider, my dear sisters, how man women are, in a discerning eye, lessened by their extravagant attachment to dress and toys, to equipage and ostentation; in a word to all the gaudy apparatus of female vanity, together with the endlessly ridiculous, no less than frequently fatal consequences, which these draw after them'[10] – are just as prescriptive as Darcy's. Both Darcy's and Collins's preconceived notions of the ideal woman hardly serve as recommendations for themselves as equal partners in marriage.

The similarity between Collins and Darcy is lost in film adaptations, with the men made into complete opposites, not just in the way they speak, but in the way they look (in spite of the fact that there is hardly any physical description of Collins in Austen's novel, save for 'He was a tall, heavy looking young man of five and twenty' (44)). In Joe Wright's 2005 adaptation, the visual differences between the two failed proposals couldn't be more pronounced. The small Tom Hollander's Collins is made even shorter by his continual slouching and bended knees, with Darcy literally head and shoulders above him. In the novel, the proposals are both set inside (significantly, Darcy proposes in Collins's house, drawing an implicit connection between the suitors), whereas in the film, Collins proposes in what Joe Wright describes on the Director's Commentary as 'the least romantic environment possible'; the large ham on the breakfast table immediately in front of Elizabeth imperceptibly equates her with a piece of meat while Collins's blue coat is the identical colour of the wall behind him, making him literally blend into the woodwork. In contrast, Wright places Darcy outside in a in a neo-classical temple in the pouring rain. The hand-held camera revolves around Darcy and Elizabeth as they draw closer and closer to each other, culminating in a near kiss, with the rain on their faces accentuating the shocked sadness experienced by both. Darcy speaks his proposal with almost indecent haste as

---

[10] James Fordyce, Sermon VIII, 'On Female Virtue, with intellectual Accomplishments', *Sermons to Young Women*, reprints from the University of Michigan Library, 1809, vol. 2, p. 8.

if he's prepared it earlier, accidentally blurting out 'I love you' in a scene which Wright describes as like a 'car crash'; it happens so quickly, it's impossible to know how to react. However, in the novel, Darcy's proposal is not dramatically presented but related to us; we are not given direct access to what Mr Darcy actually said ('He spoke well, but there were feelings besides those of the heart to be detailed, and was not more eloquent on the subject of tenderness than of pride.' (125)). Mr Darcy's incredulity at Elizabeth's refusal resembles Collins's but Elizabeth doesn't, as she does with Collins, spare the punches. She firstly accuses him of insulting her by his admission that the marriage is against his good judgement and then accuses him of ruining her sister's happiness and behaving in a dastardly manner towards Mr Wickham. His retort is to make the insults more explicit: 'Could you expect me to rejoice in the inferiority of your connections? To congratulate myself on the hope of relations, whose condition in life is so decidedly beneath my own?'(127). Darcy refers to those who Elizabeth holds most dear as socially, economically and morally inferior to himself. He speaks outside of the conventions of acceptable social behaviour and Elizabeth has no difficulty in silencing him by referring to him as un-gentlemanly. Darcy is given direct expression through his letter, produced in hindsight, in which he defends himself against Elizabeth's two accusations. Perhaps more important than the letter, is Elizabeth's response to it which Austen describes as indefinable, combining the emotions of 'astonishment, appre-hension, and even horror' (135) as Elizabeth repeatedly rereads it. In this episode, both Darcy and Elizabeth struggle and indeed fail in maintaining their politeness, a rupture that stands out in a book that is so concerned with the presentation of manners.

By far, the most famous episode in the book (possibly thanks to the 1995 adaptation, written by Andrew Davies) is Elizabeth's visit to

Pemberley where, after she has fully digested the contents of the letter and has reconsidered her earlier hostility to Darcy, she encounters him by chance. Elizabeth, while in Derbyshire with her uncle and aunt, reluctantly agrees to visit Pemberley believing the 'coast to be clear' as Darcy is away. Struck by the beauty of the landscape and the tastefulness and opulence of the house, she sees a different side of Darcy. While listening to the housekeeper praising Darcy to the skies, she gazes admiringly at his portrait that offers her a unique opportunity – for a female in the world of Jane Austen – to look without being looked at. John Wiltshire notes Elizabeth's acknowledgement of Darcy's smile 'as she had remembered to have sometimes seen' (162), asking the question, 'Why then doesn't a reader "see" Darcy smiling in the novel?'[11] The metaphor of painting is used previously in the novel when Elizabeth and Darcy are dancing at Netherfield, concluding with Elizabeth's observation that she will never have a second chance to 'sketch' Darcy: 'But if I do not take your likeness now I may never have another opportunity' (64).[12] Conversely, Darcy's sudden appearance renders both characters incapable of communication. The narrative here echoes the structure of the book as a whole: Darcy arriving causing a state of confusion, retreating and returning a much more confident and generous character. His return signals a change in the direction of the narrative, only to be thwarted a few chapters later by Elizabeth's 'bad sister', Lydia, who falls to her physical urges. The question that is playfully put before us is whether Elizabeth is in danger of succumbing to her own urges, if she falls in love with the man or the possession of the large income which,

[11] John Wiltshire, 'Mr Darcy's Smile', in Monaghan, Hudelet and Wiltshire, eds, p. 110.

[12] For a further discussion of the pictures in *Pride and Prejudice* see 'Picturing the past', pp. 77–92.

after all, as indicated in the famous opening sentence, is what every woman wants.

The visit to Pemberley is strikingly remembered in Andrew Davies' later adaptation of *Sense and Sensibity* (2008) in which Marianne comes to visit Barton Park; surveying the beauty of the park and house, she sees the shiny large piano and begins to play with an infatuated Brandon looking on. When I asked Andrew Davies about this episode in 2009, his eyes lit up and he exclaimed, yes, she falls in love with him when she sees his house and finally his 'very large instrument'. Again, this is a quintessential 'adaptation'[13] moment, but one that also recalls the 1995 adaptation and Austen's own account in *Pride and Prejudice*. It also adapts the 1995 version when the gift of the pianoforte that Marianne receives from Brandon is an obvious prelude to his proposal and completes the course of their relationship; he first views Marianne playing the piano, the close-up on his face shows his undisguised adoration of Marianne's music.

It's difficult to assert which of these novels came first given that *Pride and Prejudice* was set aside until after the publication of *Sense and Sensibility*. Elizabeth can be seen to unite the sensible Elinor and the romantic Marianne, or Elinor and Marianne can be read as splitting the two sides of Elizabeth's nature into the allegorical figures of 'sense' and 'sensibility'. The similarities between the two novels is not missed in screen adaptations as is evident in the manner in which the DVD cover of the 2005 *Pride and Prejudice* is modelled on the DVD cover for *Sense and Sensibility* (1995), both in yellow and green shades with two pictures split by the film's title, with Kiera Knightly in the same profile shot of

---

[13] See 'A timeline of *Pride and Prejudice* adaptations', pp. 12–20, for an attempt to delineate adaptation, 'the genre'.

Emma Thompson (Elinor) in the earlier film. Davies clearly adapts his own *Pride and Prejudice* in *Sense and Sensibility*, but it is blindingly obvious to anyone who has read the novel that the lack-lustre men of *Sense and Sensibility* (the 'over the hill' Colonel Brandon and the awkward and unimaginative Edward Ferrars) are transformed into more Darcy-like creations. This is even more the case in Ang Lee's 1995 film, with Alan Rickman playing a very attractive Colonel Brandon (although some may claim he's still to old for the young Marianne, played by Kate Winslett) and Hugh Grant, in the style he has become identified with, presenting an attractively romantic and quintessentially English Edward.

A survey of critical responses to *Pride and Prejudice*

Austen's reputation has developed over the last 200 years from polite approval to something, to quote Ben Jonson on Shakespeare, 'akin to idolatry' and a survey of reactions to her writing can help to account for why there are so few adaptations of *Pride and Prejudice* in the first half of the 20th century. Claire Harman notes that Austen divides readers into two distinct camps: those who love her and those who can't see the point at all, due to the restrictive nature of her subject matter.[14] The consequent moral benefits to young ladies was seen as Austen's greatest virtue in the early 19th century and her male critics were somewhat patronising in their praise or her delicacy in both style and content. The biography of Austen by her nephew James Edward Austen-Leigh perpetuated an idea of Austen as the archetypal aunt who valued equally embroidering cushions with writing novels. As Claire Harman argues in *Jane's Fame*, however, there is much evidence suppressed in

[14] Claire Harman, *Jane's Fame: How Jane Austen Conquered the World* (Edinburgh, London, New York, Melbourne: Canongate, 2009).

these accounts that points to a different Austen, one clearly bent on success as a writer and determined to attract the only readership available to her. By the mid century, writers like Charlotte Brontë and George Eliot blatantly defied the restrictions imposed upon women writers and created men who, unlike Austen's, are depicted speaking to each other without a woman present, much to the disparagement of many, such as G.K. Chesterton (1912): Austen 'could describe a man coolly; which neither George Eliot nor Charlotte Brontë could do. She knew what she knew, like a sound dogmatist'.[15] A year later, A.C. Bradley delivered his English Association lecture on Jane Austen, first given in Newnham College, Cambridge, and as Kathryn Sunderland notes, for Austen, this marks 'the beginnings of a serious academic criticism.'[16] Ignoring the restrictions imposed upon her by her position within a society that kept women in the home, her writing is dismissed as insignificant and unfeeling by D.H. Lawrence, writing in 1930:

In the old England, the curious blood-connection held the classes together . . . Already this old maid typifies 'personality' instead of character, the sharp knowing in apartness instead of knowing in togetherness, and she is to my feeling, thoroughly unpleasant, English in the bad, mean, snobbish sense of the word'.[17]

---

[15] From *The Victorian Age in Literature*, 1913, pp. 104–5, reprinted in *Jane Austen: The Critical Heritage 1870–1940*, vol. 2, ed. B.C. Southam (London and New York: Routledge & Kegan Paul, 1987), p. 239.

[16] Kathryn Sutherland, *Jane Austen's Textual Lives: from Aeschylus to Bollywood* (Oxford: Oxford University Press, 2005), p. 12.

[17] D.H. Lawrence, *Apropos of Lady Chatterley's Lover* (1930), p. 58, quoted in Southam, vol. 2, p. 107.

It's worth pausing on Lawrence's belittlement of Austen as both trivial and elitist as this is not an uncommon view of her work and one that would have barred her from the silent screen, due to its commitment to entertainment for the masses. This 'nasty' view of Austen, as a lover of money over all things is what W.H. Auden alighted on in 'His Letter to Byron' (1937):

> You could not shock her more than she shocks me;
>   Besides her Joyce seems innocent as grass.
> It makes me uncomfortable to see
>   An English spinster of the middle class
>   Describe the amorous effects of `brass',
>   Reveal so frankly and with such sobriety
>   The economic basis of society.[18]

D.W. Harding's essay 'Regulated Hatred' (1940) opens the door for Austen to enter into the English literature canon by claiming she has two types of readers: those who accept the fairytale and those who detect the irony.[19] In *The Great Tradition* (1948), F.R. Leavis 'canonised' her as 'the inaugurator of the great tradition of the English novel – and by 'great tradition' I mean the tradition to which what is great in English fiction belongs'.[20] Austen seems to have been able to tread the fine line between the popular and the classic, her admission into the canon seemingly at odds with her popularity as a writer of what is so often taken to be escapist fiction. Amidst a growing academic regard for her works, Austen also began to acquire fans as well as critics in the early 20th century: for

[18] Reprinted in Southam, vol. 2, p. 299.

[19] For a discussion of Harding's contribution to Austen scholarship, see Lynch, ed., p. 8.

[20] F.R. Leavis, *The Great Tradition* (1948; rpt. London: Penguin, 1962), p. 16.

example the Janeites emerged, an amorphous group identified largely as uncritical devotees of Austen, treating her more like a film star than a serious academic writer and the characters, as real people. Their presence can be felt on many a website today, devoted to the appreciation of Austen's writings.[21] By the late 20th century, Austen has graduated from 'charm school' in the minds of her critics, with approaches to her writing ranging from political, postcolonial to feminist readings; in fact her critical heritage is testimony to Edward Said's assertion that 'interpreting Jane Austen depends on *who* does the interpreting, *when* it is done, and no less important *where* it is done.'[22] As Devoney Looser has usefully summarised, Austen criticism now involves issues of 'authorship, class, complicity, gender, genre, history, nationality, race, resistance, and sexuality'.[23] To this list we can, of course, add film and television.

Austen's lack of sensationalism, her female focus, and her restricted class representation did not recommend her to film, known as 'the art form of democracy' in the first half of the 20th century, especially at a time when narrative which was reliant on action rather than words was more readily adaptable to silent cinema. In common with most 19th century novels, obvious problems for screen adaptation have to do with the length of the novels and the necessity of cutting minor characters and episodes. The writer's female-centred approach (famously never writing a scene without a woman in it) also poses problems for adapters given that television and film require a certain quota of men. The

---

[21] See 'Critical responses and the afterlife of the novel', pp. 130–132 for a discussion of these websites.

[22] 'Jane Austen and Empire', *Raymond Williams: Critical Perspectives*, ed. Terry Eagleton (Boston: Northeastern University Press, 1989), p. 161.

[23] Looser, ed. p. 7.

apparent need of film and television to impose closure upon narrative is another major problem facing adaptations of *Pride and Prejudice*. The ambivalence of Austen's novel will be examined in relation to the tendency in film and television to excise the political and social dimensions of the novel, in order to perpetuate the myth of Austen as a safe and undemanding author, writing in an untroubled, secure and comfortable past. Issues for adaptation are:

- Austen's language: how do adapters make a very 'wordy' novel 'visual'? This brings to mind, once again, the lack of description in Austen's fiction and the absence of her novels from the silent screen.

- How is the irony translated? Who takes over the role of narrator? Elizabeth, for example, doesn't always share the narrator's point of view as evident in the lack of self-knowledge she frequently unknowingly reveals. For example, her insistence to Collins that she's incapable of changing her mind, in hindsight, is blatantly false. The declaration, 'I am not one of those young ladies (if such young ladies there are) who are so daring as to risk their happiness on the chance of being asked a second time' (73), is perhaps one of the most ironic and troubling statements in the novel. To adapt this to screen poses quite a challenge to an adapter.

- How can the claustrophobia of the text, a featre of Austen's fiction as a whole, be made visually interesting? For instance, the pain Elizabeth feels in being so close but so far from Darcy ('He stood by her, however, for some minutes, in silence; and, at last, on the young lady's whispering to Elizabeth again, he walked away', (222)), presents a challenge for screen adaptation which is more at home with expansive rather than confined spaces.

● How is Darcy represented? Is he seen only through female eyes? The one time Elizabeth is unintentionally privy to a conversation between men ('She is tolerable; but not handsome enough to tempt *me*; and I am in no humour at present to give consequence to young ladies who are slighted by other men', (9)), is shown to have devastating consequences in the way Elizabeth behaves for the rest of the novel. The potential explosiveness and danger of unadulterated male discourse is avoided for the rest of the novel; but keeping the men at arm's length is far from viewer friendly and audiences increasingly expect the men to have equal screen time to the women.

● How is class visualised? How are the virtually invisible servants represented and what effect does this have on the narrative? Rare occasions in the novel, where we see behind closed doors, come as something of a shock to the modern reader when we realise these servants have been present all this time. Towards the end of the novel, Mrs Bennet rushes into Jane's room crying: 'My dear Jane, make haste and hurry down. He is come – Mr Bingley is come. – He is indeed . . . Here, Sarah come to Miss Bennet this moment, and help her on with her gown. Never mind Miss Lizzy's hair.' (224). The question 'who on earth is Sarah?' springs to mind and how could she be present on film for such a long time, without a single acknowledgement?[24]

● What engagement is there with the political and social dimensions of the novel? Lydia and Kitty's obsession with men in uniform is possibly made more prominent on screen where uniforms visually signify that these young men are potentially

[24] See Roger Sales, 'In Face of All the Servants: Spectators and Spies in Austen', in Lynch, ed., pp. 188–205.

engaged in fighting a war; however, the attitude of Lydia and Kitty towards the militia is damnably frivolous at times, such as the apparent pleasure they have in hearing that 'a private had been flogged' (41).

● How does Austen's representation of marriage conform to film and television expectations? Marriages in the novel (with the exception of the Gardiners) are all far from ideal and the book is punctuated by reflections on mismatches, either of convenience or of rashness.

● Parenthood, especially motherhood, is seen in a negative light. Austen's account of Mrs Bennet's triumph could possibly affect the feel-good factor of a screen ending: 'Happy for all her maternal feelings was the day on which Mrs Bennet got rid of her two most deserving daughters' (251). The word 'rid' strikes a decidedly discordant note in this sentence.

● Why is period detail normally so important in adaptations of *Pride and Prejudice*?

● The novel's origins in the epistolary tradition is apparent in the many letters in the novel, all read with eager fascination. How are these translated to screen?

Early responses to some of these dilemmas can be found in illustrations of *Pride and Prejudice*, appearing as early as 1833. In *Rethinking the Novel/Film Debate*, Kamilla Elliott looks at analogies between words and images, stemming from the tradition of *ut picture poesis*, in particular, the illustrated novel as a fore-runner of the film/literature debate and 'the interart rhetoric that speaks of prose as painting and of illustration as commentary.'[25] Illustrations,

---

[25] Kamilla Elliott, *Rethinking the Novel/Film Debate* (Cambridge: Cambridge University Press, 2003), p. 31.

like film adaptations, often result in visually concretising the characters, particularly in novels where there is so little physical description. The Richard Bentley publication (1833) includes both a frontispiece featuring the caption 'She then told him what Mr Darcy had voluntarily done for Lydia. He heard her with astonishment,'[26] and is illustrated by Elizabeth in a full and waisted dress with an elaborate hairstyle complete with ringlets and an elaborate knot perched on top of her head. A slim, youthful but balding Mr Bennet hears the news, backing away from an advancing Elizabeth. Behind him is an ornate and fully stacked book case, behind Elizabeth is an open window, visually suggesting their different personalities. The title-page features Elizabeth facing foward and Lady Catherine de Bourgh with her back to us, her left hand grasping Elizabeth's arm and her right hand raised up and pointing, accompanied by the caption, 'This is not to be bourne, Miss Bennet, I insist on being satisfied. Has he, has my nephew, made you an offer of marriage?' Elizabeth is pictured in a full-skirted dress, with a delicate foot protruding, and holding a very large parasol which encircles her face and shoulders. As early as 1833, then, Elizabeth is pictured as a modern woman with Darcy (significantly not illustrated) shrouded in mystery. These early illustrations offer us a glimpse of what is to come in the many screen adaptations of the novel, and the challenges posed in adapting Darcy (here tantalisingly both present and absent) to film and television. Hugh

[26] Jane Austen, *Pride and Prejudice* (London: Richard Bentley, 1833). These illustrations are reprinted in 1839 and 1846 (this edition includes only the frontispiece). Later illustrations, including the Routledge 1949 edition and the Hugh Thomson illustrated 1895–97 novels are discussed by Kathryn Sutherland in *Jane Austen's Textual Lives: From Aeschylus to Bollywood* (Oxford: Oxford University Press, 2005), pp. 1–10.

Thompson's one hundred, frequently whimsical, illustrations of 1894 depict Darcy for the most part with nose high in the air and in the first proposal scene, he's seen approaching a seated Elizabeth with fireplace and mirror behind him, possibly intimating both passion and vanity.[27] The frontispiece features Elizabeth 'Reading Jane's Letters', possibly in anticipation of the famous first proposal scene. The illustrations of 1902 by John Proctor in the John Dicks publication show a haughty Darcy top hat in hand, delivering the letter to Elizabeth, his face frozen in a grimace.[28] Darcy appears in a 1904 edition with the caption 'Mr Darcy declares himself', with Elizabeth seated at an open bureau, letter in hand. Darcy's head is framed with a mirror behind him, again possibly calling attention to his unacknowledged vanity.[29]

These pictures have been passed on and developed from generation to generation and the presence of the mirror makes a re-appearance in the highly acclaimed BBC adaptation of 1995 in which Darcy's face is reflected in the background while he proposes to an astonished Elizabeth. The covert message is that Darcy (memorably played by Colin Firth who came to dominate this adaptation) is at fault for speaking as much to himself as to Elizabeth and the visualisation, or concretisation of Darcy here, as in his 19th century illustrations, transforms the novel from a text in which we can only see the men through the women to one in which we can look for ourselves, seemingly without any authorial interference. But as hard as these illustrations try, they fail to

[27] Jane Austen, *Pride and Prejudice* (London: George Allen, 1894) preface George Sainsbury, illustrations, Hugh Thomson, p. 233.

[28] Jane Austen, *Pride and Prejudice* (London: John Dicks, 1902), p. 49.

[29] Jane Austen, *Pride and Prejudice* (London: Blackie and Son Limited, 1894), Illustrated by Chris. Hammond, p. 191.

compete with the novel, in the way that say John Tenniel's do with Lewis Carroll's *Alice's Adventures in Wonderland*, and possibly answer the question as to why *Pride and Prejudice* had to wait until the Sound Era to make its way to the screen.

PART 2:

From text to screen

'First impressions': the openings of screen versions of *pride and prejudice*

Austen's thematic concern with first impressions translates to screen adaptations of the novel in various ways, reflecting individual slants on the narrative, dependent on both their contexts and genres. Before examining the film and adaptations in detail and as a whole in the following sections, snapshots of the openings introduce us to the strategies each adaptation adopts in its presentation of the subject of first impressions, which is, of course, the abandoned title of the novel.

Pride and Prejudice begins with one of the most famous sentences in all of literature, 'It is a truth universally acknowledged, that a single man in possession of a good fortune, must be in a want of a wife.' The point of view here can be attributed to the ironic omniscient narrator, to Elizabeth's ironic reflection on those who think like her mother, or to the worldview of Mrs Bennet herself; all of the adaptations discussed here omit, rewrite or delay the first line of the book, creating different first impressions for their changing audiences. Recounting them here provides an opportunity to see how these 'first impressions' are hardly fresh adaptations of the novel that exist in complete isolation and, so to speak, reinvent the wheel; rather they self-consciously address each other, reflecting on, reviewing and revising what's gone before.

1940 *Pride and Prejudice*, directed Robert Z. Leonard, starring Laurence Olivier and Greer Garson

The first shot of this film is of the main street of Meryton, followed by a shot of the interior of a shop. A grovelling and sycophantic shopkeeper is the first to speak: 'Either the shell-pink gossamer muslin or the figured damask would be most becoming to your daughter Mrs Bennet'. Mrs Bennet replies: 'Now let me see, yes, yes, the pink suits you Jane and now we'll see whether the blue is becoming to you, Lizzie.' In response, the shopkeeper, exceedingly eager to make a sale holds up a piece of cloth to Mrs Bennet, Jane and Elizabeth, extolling the virtues of his prized muslin, whereupon Mrs Bennet asks: 'Is silk brocade very much worn?' This is immediately followed by a close-up of Elizabeth who responds: 'Mine is, Mama, it's been worn for three years.'

Leonard's film commences with a representation of the women as consumers, aspiring admirers of fashion, acting as a preface to the first appearance of Bingley and Darcy (who the women see moments later through the shop window). The film subtly introduces the subject of love and money and men and women as objects to be bought as property, obliquely referencing Austen's second line: 'However little known the feelings or views of such a man may be on his first entering a neighbourhood, this truth is so well fixed in the minds of the surrounding families, that he is considered as the rightful property of some one or other of their daughters' (3). Greer Garson's Elizabeth's witty one-liner is the climax of this sequence, instantly informing the viewer that she will be the star focus of this production.

1980 *Pride and Prejudice*, directed by Cyril Coke, starring Elizabeth Garvie and David Rintoul

The series begins with a shot of the Bennets' house, followed by a man pulling a horse and cart laden with luggage. Mary runs out to receive news and then rushes back to the house, with Charlotte passing her on the lawn, about to make a call on the Bennet family. The scene moves to inside and a conversation between Charlotte and Elizabeth, with Charlotte the first to speak: 'His name is Mr Bingley. He is unmarried and well under thirty. What a wonder! A single man in possession of a good fortune coming to live at Netherfield'. Elizabeth quickly replies: 'It is a truth universally acknowledged that such a man must be in want of a wife', with Charlotte responding in a reworking of the second line of the novel: 'Of course, he is the rightful property of one or other of the neighbourhood daughters.' Elizabeth's attempt to qualify Charlotte's observation, 'However little is known of his character, Charlotte', is met with Charlotte's assertive retort: 'Little need be known, Eliza. Happiness in marriage is entirely a matter of chance. It is best to know as little as possible of the defects of the person with whom you're to pass your life.' Elizabeth, smiles in denial: 'You make me laugh, Charlotte. But it is not sound. You know it is not sound and that you would never act that way yourself. Never'. Charlotte wryly retorts: 'Did your mother know Mr Bennet before she married him? Did he know her?' with Elizabeth conceding: 'You are too shrewd, Charlotte. Then my father is remarkable. So odd a mixture of quick parts and caprice that even after twenty years, my mother still fails to understand him. Her mind is less difficult to comprehend.'

The only man in sight in the opening of this adaptation is the faceless driver of the luggage cart, preparing us for a reading of the novel that keeps men at a distance. The clash between the sensibilities of Charlotte and Elizabeth introduces the series but with

Elizabeth significantly offering no alternative to Charlotte's material-istic view of marriage. Elizabeth's final words in this exchange make explicit what is diluted in most of the later adaptations, focussing on the unequal and possibly unhappy marriage of her own parents.

1995 *Pride and Prejudice*, directed by Simon Langton, starring Colin Firth and Jennifer Ehle

The series opens with a close-up of horses' hooves, then a midshot of two men on horseback galloping across the countryside and stopping with a stately home in the distance. Mr Bingley is the first to speak, 'It's a fair prospect', with Darcy responding, 'Pretty enough, I grant you'. Bingley continues: 'It's nothing to Pemberley, I know. But I must settle somewhere. Have I your approval?' Avoiding a direct answer, Darcy observes, 'You'll find the society something savage' and Bingley knowingly retorts: 'Country manners? I think they're charming'. Darcy, with a trace of irritation in his voice, tries to wind up the debate, 'Then you better take it', and Bingley concludes, 'Thank you, I shall. I shall close with my attorney directly'. The conversation is followed by a shot of Elizabeth in closeup, watching the men galloping in the distance.

The opening is almost a mirror opposite of the earlier BBC adaptation with the men rather than the women surveying the scene, contrasting the different attitudes of Bingley and Darcy, one the enthusiast and the other, the sceptic. Darcy's 'first impressions' of Netherfield prepare us for his first impressions of Elizabeth ('Pretty enough, I grant you') and the men's conversation about taking Netherfield anticipates the compromises of the novel's ending, with both men having 'to settle somewhere' in spite of a society that can be perceived as 'savage'.

2001, *Bridget Jones's Diary*, directed by Sharon Maguire, starring Renée Zellweger and Colin Firth

The film opens with Bridget emerging from a car in a snowy scene, walking towards the camera accompanied by a voiceover: 'It all began on New Year's Day in my thirty-second year of being single.' A 'Christmas-card' shot of a small village covered in snow with a wreath placed on a memorial in the foreground is presented with the voiceover: 'Once again I found myself on my own and going to my mother's annual turkey curry buffet. Every year she tries to fix me up with some bushy-haired, middle-aged bore and I feared this year would be no exception.' Bridget is seen from behind in front of a house with her mother opening the door, beaming: 'There you are, dumpling!'

The film's use of *Pride and Prejudice* is only apparent in the mother's addiction to matchmaking and the heroine's veiled confession about her fear of spinsterhood, visually offset by the Christmas setting, conveying to the audience that something good is about to happen.

2003 *Pride and Prejudice: A Latter Day Comedy*, directed by Andrew Black, starring Kam Heskin and Orlando Seale

A blank screen and voiceover of an American female introduce this film with: 'It is a truth universally acknowledged that a girl of a certain age and in a certain situation in life must be in want of a husband. And I guess I was in that situation and according to my mother, I had passed that age quite some time ago.' A birthday cake comes into focus, one candle extinguished and the voiceover continues: 'I suppose they only sell candles in packs of twenty four.' A girl watching (Jane) comes into focus, accompanied by the voiceover: 'Still, it was nice of the girls to remember.' This follows an introduction and brief description of the birthday party crowd, including Jane, Lydia and Austen her pet dog, Kitty, Mary and finally, Elizabeth herself.

Immediately we find ourselves in familiar *Pride and Prejudice* territory, transplanted to the genre of teenpic, with a friendship rather than family group. Elizabeth is the last to come into focus and appears plainly dressed wearing glasses, openly confessing like Bridget Jones and unlike Austen's Elizabeth Bennet, her fear that she is in danger of becoming 'over the hill'.

2004 *Bride and Prejudice*, directed by Gurinder Chadha, starring Aishwarya Rai and Martin Henderson

The film opens with a shot of the Golden Temple accompanied by a line from a prayer sung in Punjabi. While the credits are rolling, an aerial shot of Lalita (Elizabeth) making notes in a book on the back of a tractor within an immense sun baked field is interspersed with shots of a plane landing and collecting luggage from a tractor, then Lalita, at the end of her journey, handing her notes to her father. Darcy, Balraj (Bingley) and Kiran (Caroline Bingley) are seen getting into a taxi, with crowded street scenes surrounding them. Darcy is the first to speak: 'This is mayhem. This is like Bedlam.' His companion, Balraj, replies, 'Good isn't it?', to which Darcy answers, 'What do you mean, it's a bit like New York?' Kiran then quips: 'Better get used to it, Darcy. We're here for two weeks.' A dismayed looking Darcy concludes: 'Jesus, Balraj, where the hell have you brought me?' The scene changes to a shot of a man with a watering can in front of a grand but run-down house. A woman is heard shouting off screen, 'Hurry up, you silly girls', followed by a shot of the mother (Manorama Bakshi) inside who is loudly proclaiming: 'We must make sure Jaya meets this Mr Balraj from London before anyone else'. Following a shot of the mother and two girls inside getting dressed is a midshot of Lalita and Jaya, back to back getting ready. Lalita responds to her mother's urgency, for Jaya's ears alone: 'All mothers think that any single guy with big bucks must be shopping for a wife.' Jaya answers back: 'I'm embarrassed to say, but I hope he is.' Lalita looks a little shocked and asks, 'What, shopping or loaded?' to which Jaya responds: 'Well, both.'

Cultural differences between hero and heroine are immediately highlighted and a contrast is drawn between vast expanses of countryside with the business of the crowded cityscape in the opening sequence. Lalita is seen before Darcy but speaks after him, rephrasing Austen's opening line. It is for her sister – rather than Lalita – to articulate the semi-desperation of the plight of the single woman, as articulated by the earlier modernised versions of the novel.

2005 *Pride & Prejudice*, directed by Joe Wright, starring Kiera Knightley and Matthew Macfadyen

The sound of birdsong and shot of the sun rising above trees open this film. Elizabeth in midshot is seen walking while reading a book, followed by a closeup of the book, astutely described by Carol M. Doyle as 'curiously yellowed with age'.[1] Elizabeth sighs and closes it having come to the end. A steadicam shot follows her across a bridge, passing some hanging laundry and poultry, accompanied by piano music. Mary is revealed from behind in the house, playing

[1] 'Carol M. Doyle, Jane Austen and Mud: *Pride & Prejudice* (2005), British Realism and the Heritage Film', *Persuasions On-line* 27 (2), 2007, p. 5/10, http://www.jasna.org/persuasions/on-line/vol27no2/dole.htm. Accessed 8/05/10.

the piano and what seems to be non-diegetic music crosses over to diegetic. Lydia, Kitty and Jane enter the frame and Jane is first to speak, reproaching her sister: 'Lydia!' Shots of a table strewn with bonnets and sewing things and a servant seen from the house outside feeding geese follow. Elizabeth is then seen from outside a window, overhearing her mother: 'My dear Mr Bennet, have you heard? Netherfield Park is let at last. Do you not want to know who has taken it?' Mr Bennet replies: 'As you wish to tell me, my dear, I doubt I have any choice in the matter.' Elizabeth enters the house and joins her sisters and rebukes Kitty for listening at the door.

Unlike the previous openings discussed above, this film begins with Elizabeth, following her point of view up the garden path, gradually introducing us to her life. She is distinguished from the rest of her family, as she is seen from the outside looking in, an observer, reader and perhaps even controller of her life (since the book she is reading, as will be discussed in *Pride and Prejudice* as concealed autobiography', pp. 109–122, is, as only the most observant viewers will recognise, none other than *Pride and Prejudice* itself).

2007 *Becoming Jane*, directed by Julian Jarrold, starring Anne Hathaway and James McAvoy

Jarrold's film begins with a succession of shots including a panoramic view of the English countryside,[2] an elegant hand holding a pen at a writing desk, a closeup of a clock face, a rusty tap with water slowly dripping, all accompanied by a birdsong. Jane is heard quietly uttering words while writing, followed by a shot of the vicarage, a medium shot of Jane through double doors at a piano, a closeup of fingers on piano keys, a shot of Jane in a night-dress looking forlornly out of a window, shots, through a window, of

[2] The film was actually shot in Ireland.

Cassandra sleeping and Mr and Mrs Austen asleep, shot of a sow suckling her piglets, a woman approaching the house, closeup of Jane writing and then reading her work and the female servant entering with a washing tray. Jane starts playing loudly, the servant drops her tray on the stairs, the sow and her piglets are disturbed and we see birds in a flutter. Mr and Mrs Austen wake up, Casssandra and her fiancé meet in their nightdresses in the hallway. Robert (Cassandra's fiancé) asks: 'What is it?' Cassandra answers: 'Jane'. A shot of Eliza (Jane's cousin) reading follows and then we see the couple retreating to their rooms; Robert smiles, and Cassandra giggles once the door is closed behind her. A shot follows of Mr and Mrs Austen waking up and Mrs Austen screaming: 'Jane!'

The rupture to the tranquillity of a seemingly ordinary family caused by a reflective Jane introduces this biopic adaptation of *Pride and Prejudice*. The viewer is immediately made aware of the likelihood that this central figure is going to make a difference to her world.

2008, *Lost in Austen*, directed by Dan Zeff, starring Jemima Rooper and Elliot Cowan

A zoom into a closeup of the central character, bank clerk Amanda Price, facing the camera opens the four-part series. In voiceover, Amanda proclaims: 'I have no right to complain about my life.' This is followed by a sequence of shots, from Amanda's point of view, of a man before her, waving arms excitedly and shouting, 'I want this account dejointed, right, I want her name gone', with Amanda's voiceover, 'I mean, it's the same for everybody and I do what we all do'. The next shots reveal a couple with a man on a mobile asking 'Did you get the sack?', a mother shouting at a baby in a pushchair, with Amanda's voiceover, 'And

I do what we all do, I take it on the chin, and patch myself up with Jane Austen'. A shot of Amanda with a book on an overcrowded tube is followed by a shot of St Paul's, followed by a shot of Amanda, carrying shopping, walking at night. The voiceover continues: 'I know I sound like a terrible loser, I mean, I do actually have a boyfriend, it's just sometimes I'd rather stay in with Elizabeth Bennet.' Amanda is then seen in her flat with a closeup of a ringing mobile, reading 'Michael calling'.

Amanda's desire for escape is explained by the coarseness of the 21st century world that surrounds her, culminating in the closeup of the mobile phone, which epitomises her boyfriend as nothing other than technological convenience. The opening lures viewers in with a promise of escape into a better world and the assumption that Amanda makes, that the past is much friendlier and homelier than the present.

Conspicuously missing from all of these adaptations of the opening of *Pride and Prejudice*, with the possible exception of *Lost in Austen* in its interrogation of the theme of escape, is any hint of the political context of the novel. Instead, the preoccupation of most of these screen *Pride and Prejudice*s is essentially with gender and a reiteration of what is often regarded as central to the novel's popularity: the 'timeless' desire to achieve happiness through a marriage of equal minds. Bringing these adaptations, thankfully still available on video, DVD and YouTube, head to head, enables viewers and readers to ask and answer questions based on a range of issues to do with gender, politics, class, production values, genre, audience expectations and media specificity and to ponder just how one novel can tell so many stories.

'A striking resemblance?': *pride and prejudice* on television

Those involved in television adaptation of *Pride and Prejudice*, at least up until the late 20th century, have continually expressed a commitment to fidelity, aiming to achieve what Austen herself describes as 'a striking resemblance' to the original. A common theme of the publicity surrounding the adaptations and the reviews of these productions is the attention to detail, in both the preservation of Austen's language or her 'intentions', and the care taken in the reconstruction of the Regency period in which the novel was produced. Whatever we think of this quest for authenticity, it's undeniable that it's doomed to failure, as watching the adaptations in hindsight, what is striking is what they give away about their own periods, rather than what is revealed about Austen's, whether it be in the cut of the costume, the make-up, the quality of the production, or the particular slant taken on the novel.

For most of the 20th century, Austen's second home seems to be television. While there are five mainstream hit and miss film adaptations of *Pride and Prejudice*, 1940, 2003, 2004 (*Bride and Prejudice*), 2005 and 2007 (*Becoming Jane*), there are several television adaptations (1938, 1952, 1958, 1967, 1980, 1995), all of which have been popularly received, and this section will consider how the episodic nature of Austen's narrative is, on the whole, more appealing to television than film; like the experience of reading, television series are taken in instalments, prolonging the pleasure of the text, providing lengthy pauses between each episode to reflect on what's going to happen next.

'Straight' adaptations of *Pride and Prejudice* have appeared on television at least once a decade since the beginning of the Sound Era. While each of these adaptations appropriates the novel for different audiences, they all paradoxically cling to their own notions of historical fidelity. Andrew Davies' achievement of changing the centre of the narrative from Elizabeth to the enigmatic and attractive Darcy seems to have ground to a halt the steady stream of 'straight' *Pride and Prejudice* adaptations on television. While there have been plenty of take-offs of the novel (such as *Lost in Austen*), Davies' adaptation has stood its position, becoming, at least temporarily, the 'definitive' version. What it offers to us is a break from the past and attempts in the latter half of the 20th century, especially in literary criticism, to appropriate the novel as a feminist text, no more apparent than in the adaptation immediately preceding it: Fay Weldon's adaptation of 1980.

This distinctly feminist version of the text was released in 1980, directed by Cyril Coke amidst what the then BBC Head of Drama, Jonathan Powell has described as the turf wars of the British Broadcasting Company and Independent Television. While ITV was airing the innovative, visually stunning, *Brideshead Revisited* (1981), the BBC competed with *Tinker, Tailor, Soldier, Spy* (1979) and *Smiley's People* (1982). Best known for the charismatic understatement displayed by the protagonist, Sir Alec Guinness, these provided a more modern contrast to *Brideshead*. The latter is remembered for *tour de force* performances from Sir John Gielgud and Sir Laurence Olivier, and a meandering nostalgic fetishisation of Oxford in the 1930s. Both adaptations were remarkable as they changed the face of television drama, the location shooting immersing television viewers in a more immediate filmic experience. In contrast to these productions is *Pride and Prejudice* which retains what was expected of a BBC adaptation of this vintage in its staid theatrical sets, nonetheless featuring meticulously recreated Regency interiors and panoramic views of the archetypal English landscape in the height of summer. As Jonathan Powell, BBC Head of Drama, recalls it was chosen as a safe bet:

> Here's a little anecdote, though, which puts the Andrew Davies P and P in context, plus the other recent dramatisations of Jane Austen.
>
> We, that is Betty Willingale and I, were having a bit of trouble persuading our Head of Department to let us do *Crime and Punishment*, as I recall. The problem was the Russian names. His view was that the audience never watched Russian dramatisation because all the names of the characters were too long and ended in '....ov', which meant they couldn't tell who was who.
>
> Anyway, some time around then – I was the New Boy at the BBC – I asked Betty what we did if we had a string of productions which didn't do well or which the critics didn't like or which suffered from being, as people used to say in those days, caviar to the general.
>
> Quick as a flash Betty replied, 'Don't worry. If we are ever in trouble for not being populist enough with our choices, we just do *Pride and Prejudice*. The audience always turns up for that.' And then she added 'or maybe we resurrect *How Green Is My Valley*.[1]

[1] Email: Jonathan Powell to Deborah Cartmell 20/10/09.

But what doesn't seem so 'safe' is the choice of feminist novelist, Fay Weldon as screenwriter and while *Brideshead* and *Smiley's People* focus on male roles and the construction of masculinity, this is a very female-centred adaptation. Weldon's current brand of compromising feminism typified by her offhand comment, 'It's easier to pick up your husband's socks and clean the loo'[2] than make a fuss, sums up this adaptation of Austen's novel where the women, clearly superior to the men, succumb resignedly to the pressures of a flawed patriarchal society. The reading of the novel is very much in line with Mary Poovey's analysis of *Pride and Prejudice* in which Elizabeth has, in some degree, to accept the mortification to her vanity in Darcy's first reaction to her: 'Yet the juxtaposition of Elizabeth's lively wit with this pretentious and repressive society cuts both ways; for if the vacuity of her surroundings highlights her energy, it also encourages her to cultivate her natural vivacity beyond its legitimate bounds.'[3]

The adaptation is littered with references to the literature of this period, Mr Darcy is compared to 'Byron himself', Colonel Fitzwilliam recommends *The Edinburgh Review* (a magazine, with reformist views, founded in 1802) to Elizabeth, a familiarity with the writings of William Godwin and Mary Wollstonecraft is revealed by Elizabeth, and Darcy playfully asks Mr Gardiner when talking about fishing if he is indeed '*The Compleat Angler*' (referring to Izaac Walton's treatise on fishing, first published in 1653). While this adaptation doesn't go in for innovative shooting or filmic effects, particularly

[2] Interview by Bryony Gordon, *The Daily Telegraph*, 26 August 2009, http://www.telegraph.co.uk/culture/books/authorinterviews/6089253/Fay-Weldon-Its-easier-to-pick-up-your-husbands-socks-and-clean-the-loo.html. Accessed 21/10/09.

[3] Mary Poovey, *The Proper Lady and the Woman Writer: Ideology as Style in the Works of Mary Wollstonecraft, Mary Shelley, and Jane Austen* (Chicago: University of Chicago Press, 1984), p.195.

striking is Darcy's delivery of his letter to Elizabeth; as she reads it he is seen to be retreating slowly away in the distance, visually becoming increasingly remote from her in contrast to her growing esteem for him, as revealed by her widening eyes. As she reads he literally becomes more and more unreachable.

Eclipsed by Andrew Davies' 1995 *Pride and Prejudice*, the earlier series has much to recommend it. Mr Collins (played by Malcolm Rennie), like an estate agent, is seen constantly measuring up Longbourn in anticipation of his proposal to one of the sisters. Darcy, played by David Rintoul, is strikingly remote and statuesque (in fact, hardly moving his lips in the rare occasions in which he speaks) until he comes alive in his second proposal to Elizabeth, physically becoming more animated, relaxed, almost bursting to talk after such a sustained and painful silence. Visually he's transformed into a new man (one even, with a feminine side), someone who Elizabeth can actually talk to. The narrative insinuates that Darcy needs Elizabeth to be 'complete' rather than Elizabeth needing Darcy. Elizabeth, played by Elizabeth Garvie, while 23 at the time of filming, looks older and wiser than her years, marking her visually sensible, to be trusted, and accordingly, an Austen stand-in. Irene Richard, who plays Charlotte, goes on to play Elinor in *Sense and Sensibility* in the following year, reflecting her association with good sense and the triumph of materialism over romanticism. As has been noted by Deborah Moggach, screenwriter of *Pride and Prejudice*, 2005, Mrs Bennet (played by Priscilla Morgan) in this adaptation becomes the unsung heroine of the piece.[4] Moray Watson's Mr Bennet's abdication of power at the beginning of the story is visually notable with Mrs Bennet, in contrast, having to do all the work and take over in conducting the girls to the Assembly ball where she

[4] 3rd Annual Association of Literature on Screen Studies, Amsterdam, September, 2008.

gallantly stands up for Elizabeth when slighted by Darcy: 'You lose nothing', she chirps. Mrs Bennet is always busy, albeit if it's only to rearrange porcelain figures on the mantelpiece, while Mr Bennet rarely gets out of his chair, where his main occupation is to whinge. In marked contrast to the visually static men, the activity of the women is emphasised throughout this production; Mrs Gardiner, for instance, is seen to be studying a collection of herbal specimens prior to the unexpected arrival of Darcy at the inn at Lambton. That it's a female focussed adaptation is evident from the video/DVD cover which positions Elizabeth and Jane in the foreground, with a smaller Elizabeth and Darcy a few paces behind; the signal here is clearly that the adaptation privileges the relationship of the sisters above that of the obligatory heterosexual pairing of Darcy and Elizabeth, reminding us that Elizabeth's original knee-jerk rejection of Darcy is out of fidelity to her sister, explicitly choosing sisterhood over marriage. Indeed this adaptation comes the closest of all late 20th to early earlier 21st century adaptations to questioning the hetero-normative values of the novel itself.

Privileging the relationships of the women over the men, in this adaptation, can be regarded in the light of critical questioning over Jane Austen's own sexuality; the fact that she never married and that her novels dwell almost entirely on the female experience have inspired readings of the novels as covertly lesbian. For instance, if we didn't know she was writing to her niece, Fanny, it is easy to attribute Austen's chosen terms of endearment, as directed at a lover rather than a member of her family: 'You are inimitable, irresistible. You are the delight of my Life . . . I shall hate you when your delicious play of Mind is all settled down into conjugal & maternal affections.'[5] Claudia L. Johnson, in her comprehensive

[5] 'To Fanny Knight, Thursday 20–Friday 21 February 1817 Chawton', *Pride and Prejudice*, ed. Gray, p. 280.

account of the history of this alternative reading of Austen's novels, compares the reaction to Austen as potentially lesbian to the shock at the discovery that Cary Grant – icon of masculinity – was actually gay. Johnson describes this clash of assumptions (which she illustrates has a long history) peaking in 1995 in an article in *The London Review of Books* by Terry Castle entitled, 'Was Jane Austen Gay?' Johnson is worth quoting at length here:

> But no one expected the vehemence that followed as scores of people rushed to rescue Austen from the charge of 'sister love': one reader, assuming that 'Terry' was a man, damned the 'drip-drip' smuttiness of 'his' discussions of women's familiarity; some swore up and down that marriages in Austen's novels were perfectly felicitous without requiring the supplemental pleasures of sororal love; others insisted testily, if inanely, that since sisters commonly shared beds in those days, it is anachronistic to imply that their intimacy meant anything 'more'. Austen scholar B.C. Southam entered the fray: does Austen describe women's bodies with 'homophilic fascination,' as Castle suggested? Not to worry: Austen was an amateur seamstress and thus had a perfectly innocent reason for attending to how gowns hugged the persons of her female acquaintance . . . Vainly did Castle plead that she had never asserted the existence of an incestuously lesbian relationship between Austen and her sister: the words *homophilic* and *homoerotic* provoked readers to announce that the limits of tolerance had been reached. Castle had 'polluted the shrine' and this would not be suffered.[6]

---

[6] 'The Divine Miss Jane: Jane Austen, Janeites, and the Discipline of Novel Studies', in Lynch, ed., p. 27.

The backgrounding of the courtship plot in the 1980 adaptation also reflects readings, such as that of W.H. Auden in his poem, 'she shocks me',[7] that point to Austen's romantic cynicism in which money wins over romance. It's very much an open question in this adaptation as to how ironic Elizabeth is in her explanation of how she fell in love – 'It has been coming on so gradually, that I hardly know when it began. But I believe I must date it from my first seeing his beautiful grounds at Pemberley' (244). Although her tongue is in her cheek, the element of truth in the statement could be regarded as not only a triumph of materialism over romanticism, but an acknowledgement that a man can be tolerated only if he brings with him the compensation of wealth.

Articulation of Elizabeth's admiration for Pemberley is delayed in this version until after she has seen the house, its contents, and its grounds. When asked by a very commanding Mrs Gardiner whether she likes the place, Elizabeth replies, 'Oh yes. I've never seen a place for which nature has done so much or where natural beauty has been so little counteracted by an awkward taste', adapting the omniscient narrator's lines at the beginning of the first chapter of Volume 3. Elizabeth is not as flappable as her successors. It is her eloquence and superior society that is the object of Darcy's attraction; the banal chatter of his party: 'I find mountains to be very dull, they lack refinement'; 'I can't abide a mountain', is in direct contrast to the conversation of Elizabeth and the Gardiners.

The attention to period detail and the declared intention to observe the utmost fidelity to the novel is taken up 15 years later by the BBC and the new series was eagerly anticipated by the press as the series producer Sue Birtwhistle recalls:

[7] See 'The novel and its reputation', p. 38.

The project may have been 'on hold', but the publicity wasn't. Andrew (Davies) had been asked in an interview what he was currently writing. He mentioned *Pride and Prejudice* and, in the same sentence, the words 'sex and money'. The tabloid newspapers needed no further encouragement. 'SEX ROMP JANE AUSTEN' hit the headlines. This new version, they confidentally asserted, would have full frontal nudity and daring sex scenes.[8]

Adapted by Andrew Davies and directed by Simon Langton this version continues to trump previous and subsequent adaptations of the novel, for the most part, due to the transformation of Darcy, played by Colin Firth. While it's clear from the DVD featurette, *The Making of Pride and Prejudice*, that every effort was made to be 'true to the text', this is an adaptation with a twist. Filming rather than video recording makes for a different kind of production with costumes, locations, and interiors meticulously and lavishly presented. Time passing is conveyed throughout the series, with the changing seasons and the corresponding change in costumes.

In contrast to the 1980s' Mrs Bennet, the infantilisation of Mrs Bennet (albeit skilfully played by Alison Steadman) is perhaps the most annoying aspect of this adaptation. Her childish behaviour and almost cartoon-like movements, remove any remnant of credibility she might have been given in the novel. Dressed almost like a baby, in clothes clearly designed to desexualise her, we first see her desperately trying to keep up with Mr Bennet on their way to church, unable to repress her excitement about the letting of Netherfield Hall. Visual associations with Jemima Puddleduck come to mind, as she resembles a squawking duck, with her chicks

---

[8] Sue Birtwhistle, *The Making of 'Pride and Prejudice'* (Harmondsworth: Penguin, BBC, 1995), p. vi.

reluctantly following behind. The association is taken a stage further in later adaptations; the *mise en scène* of the opening sequence of the 2005 film literally contains ducks and geese as a visual correlative to the Bennet family and in *Becoming Jane* (2007), the Austen family are juxtaposed in the opening sequence of the film with a sow suckling her piglets. Unlike the 1980 adaptation, there is no doubt as to the superiority of Mr Bennet over his wife, and this is in keeping with the adaptation as a whole, in which the men are almost invariably placed, both physically and metaphorically, before the women. While denying this male-centred reading, in *The Making of 'Pride and Prejudice,'* Andrew Davies, in bringing it to our attention, also affirms it:

> I realise in telling this story that I've really been telling it rather as if it's a story about Mr Darcy, whereas the book is definitely a book about Elizabeth. In the novel Darcy is a mysterious, unpredictable character, whom we only really begin to under-stand right at the end. I haven't done a version about Mr Darcy, but I suppose in showing that his desire for Elizabeth is the motivation of the plot, I've perhaps pushed it a bit more to being a story about Elizabeth and Darcy, rather than a story about Elizabeth.[9]

The opening shot with Bingley and Darcy galloping in the direction of Netherfield, watched by Elizabeth, sets the tone for the entire production with the men very much the objects of the female gaze. The series is punctuated with Darcy gazing at Elizabeth while at the same time he himself is a subject of the viewer's gaze, culminating in the famous scene in the lake, the living embodiment

[9] Ibid, pp. 3–4.

of the perfect picture Elizabeth has been looking at in Pemberley. Darcy is pictured again in a mirror in Elizabeth's bedroom while she muses about the loss of his good opinion. Possibly inspired by earlier book illustrations, the mirror is significantly present in Darcy's first proposal in which, while ostensibly addressing Elizabeth, the presence of his reflection intimates that his primary concern is with himself. The series literally makes Darcy into a living portrait for the delectation of both Elizabeth and the viewer. Davies' intention to put the men back in the novel is apparent in interpolations where we see Darcy alone: fresh from the bath, looking out of his window at Elizabeth, or engaged in a fencing bout, explicitly to relieve his sense of frustration at the conflict between his head and his heart, caused by both his uncontrollable love for Elizabeth and his failure to gain her affection.

This rendition of the visit to Pemberley has been extensively covered in accounts of Austen on screen. H. Elisabeth Ellington has noted the romantic (rather than materialistic) attraction of Elizabeth to the house insofar as the script downplays Elizabeth's attractions to Darcy's possessions by giving most of Austen's lines about the beauty of Pemberley's surroundings to the Gardiners. The filmmakers shy away from presenting Elizabeth at Pemberley as Austen presents her, consuming the view from Darcy's window with 'something like regret'.[10]

It is impossible to talk about this adaptation without touching upon the phenomenon of 'Darcymania' (seemingly coexisting with 'Austenmania') that swept the news immediately following its release. The adulation for Colin Firth's Darcy as smouldering

---

[10] H. Elisabeth Ellington, 'A Correct Taste in the Landscape: Pemberley as Fetish and Commodity', *Jane Austen in Hollywood*, eds Linda Troost and Sayre Greenfield (1998; 2nd ed; Lexington: University of Kentucky Press, 2001), p. 102.

romantic hero continues to be expressed on fan sites, seemingly refusing to go away. 'The Friends of Firth Scrapbook Periodicals Page' sums up the effect Firth's portrayal has had in generating and maintaining his fans:

Imagine, for a moment, that you are in the grand ballroom of an imposing Georgian mansion. As you whirl around the room, dancing with an enchanting young man, you bask in a sumptuous atmosphere lit by chandeliers and candelabras and augmented by attendants in costumes and wigs. Surveying a group of dark-suited gentlemen in the corner, you spot a sullen-faced man fiddling nervously with his exquisitely embroidered lace cravat. His brooding eyes challenge your curious stare, and you feel as if his piercing gaze has penetrated the very depths of your soul. By a stroke of luck, his best friend introduces you to him. But before a single word can escape from your lips, your new acquaintance leaves the room and gallops away, his horse madly tearing through the streets. The amazed crowd whispers nervously, but your only thought is of the mysterious gentleman . . . Does this remind you of how you felt after watching the BBC's adaptation of *Pride and Prejudice* on A& E? Admit it. You've got 'Darcy Fever'. The handsomely sulky Mr Darcy, played by British actor Colin Firth, is the latest in a long line of sexy stars this movie season. Move over, George Clooney. Step aside, Pierce Brosnan. Firth's brooding hero has got women in two continents wild over Jane Austen's wittiest and funniest novel in ways that poor Jane would never have imagined. Unfortunately, Firth doesn't take it all off in *Pride and Prejudice* – but mind you, there are plenty of erotic scenes to go around.'[11]

[11] http://www.friendsoffirth.com/periodicals/96chi.html. Accessed 26/03/10.

The fact that Darcy doesn't strip off entirely in the lake sequence, as originally intended, makes this episode more tantalising and exciting to viewers. Arguably as sexy as Darcy's strip and swim is the first sight of Pemberley where Elizabeth and the Gardiners slowly progress through the park, keenly anticipating their first view of the house. The presentation of Pemberley is evoked in a manner that captures the latent eroticism – if it can be called that – of Austen's description of Elizabeth's first impression of the estate in Volume 3, Chapter 1:

> Elizabeth, as they drove along, watched for the first appearance of Pemberley Woods with some perturbation; and when at length they turned in at the lodge, her spirits were in a high flutter.
>
> The park was very large, and contained great variety of ground. They entered it in one of its lowest points, and drove for some time through a beautiful wood, stretching over a wide extent. Elizabeth's mind was too full for conversation, but she saw and admitted every remarkable spot and point of view. They gradually ascended for half a mile, and then found themselves at the top of a considerable eminence, where the wood ceased, and the eye was instantly caught by Pemberley House, situated on the opposite side of a valley, into which the road with some abruptness wound. It was a large, handsome building, standing well on rising ground, and backed by a ridge of high woody hills; – and in front, a stream of some natural importance was swelled into greater, but without any artificial appearance. Its banks were neither formal, nor falsely adorned. Elizabeth was delighted. She had never seen a place for which nature had done more, or where natural beauty had been so little counteracted by an awkward taste. They were all of them

> warm in their admiration; and at that moment she felt, that to be
> mistress of Pemberley might be something! (p.159)

Following John Barrell's approach to John Clare,[12] H. Elisabeth
Ellington demonstrates how this seemingly vague account is 'in
fact, a highly detailed description of the perfect late eighteenth-
century landscape garden. Influenced by theories of the
Picturesque and the rise of landscape painting, landowners were
at great pains to conceal their houses along the approach until a
'considerable eminence' was reached which would afford a
commanding view of the property, transforming the land into a
picture.'[13] The description of Pemberley is in many ways the moral
centre of the novel, the meeting place of Austen's central
concerns with artificiality and nature, sense and sensibility, society
and the individual, the marriage of art and nature. But this passage,
possibly, is also one of the inspirations behind the sexually explicit
'mashup', *Pride and Promiscuity: The Lost Sex Scenes of Jane
Austen* (Arielle Eckstut, 2003) in its erotic suggestiveness. The novel
makes explicit the implicit eroticism of the Davies' adaptation,
showing how the banality of the conversation – and the
descriptions – masks what's actually going on:

> He made no immediate answer, but outlined the edge of her
> muslim frock and slowly dipped his fingertips beneath the fabric.
> Elizabeth did not move, but closed her eyes and felt the colour
> again rise to her cheeks. Her face was deeply flushed, and when
> she opened her eyes, she saw that his was no less so.

[12] John Barrell, *The Idea of Landscape and the Sense of Place, 1730–1840: An
Approach to the Poetry of John Clare* (Cambridge: Cambridge University Press,
1972).

[13] Troost and Greenfield, eds, p. 99.

'Let us talk, Miss Elizabeth Bennet,' he said, now pressing the length of his body full against hers, 'about the weather'.[14]

The anticipation followed by the excitement of the revelation of the house in Austen's novel has almost a Lawrencian flavour; Elizabeth gradually ascends from the 'lowest point' to the 'top of a considerable eminence' upon which Pemberley suddenly becomes visible. Austen's choice of details, the *rising ground* upon which the house is positioned, the *swelling* stream in front, and the *warmth* Elizabeth feels upon its appearance, makes this among Austen's most sexually charged descriptions. And the house, of course, is the reflection of Darcy himself, preparing us for Elizabeth's change of mind. This section of the novel is also remarkable in depicting late 18th, early 19th century tourism and the penchant for visiting grand country houses, a taste for which is more than manifest in the heritage genre of adaptation, of which the 1995 television adaptation of *Pride and Prejudice* is prime example, if not *the* prime example. The journey to Pemberley in this version takes on a quest-like dimension, the arrival at which is the climactic and defining moment of the series.

Pemberley is revealed to us as if it's being undressed in Simon Langton's direction of this scene. In the midst of a discussion as to when the party is going to reach the house, Mrs Gardiner suddenly gasps 'wait' and the mood changes, with the non-diegetic music becoming quieter, accompanied by a view of trees whose branches, curtain-like, are drawn from right to left slowly unveiling a full view of the magnificent Pemberley in its naked beauty. The reaction shot that immediately follows shows Elizabeth breathing heavily through shock and admiration; and the house, to put it

[14] Arielle Eckstut, *Pride and Promiscuity: The Lost Sex Scenes of Jane Austen* (Edinburgh: Canongate, 2003), p. 27.

crudely, becomes an erection in both senses of the word. The banter between the Gardiners and Elizabeth about the discrepancy between the house and the owner invites the viewer to consider the opposite: the house and the owner as being one and the same, reinforced with Mrs Gardiner suggesting 'perhaps the beauty of the house renders its owner a little less repulsive'. The connection between the house and the man is made explicit with the camera cutting between scenes of Elizabeth and the Gardiners inside the house and Darcy outside, ferociously galloping towards his estate. Echoing Elizabeth's breathlessness upon the sight of Pemberley, Darcy stops and gets off his horse while the film cuts to Elizabeth viewing the larger portrait of Darcy which metamorphoses into Darcy himself, removing his outer clothes (Davies originally wanted Darcy to strip off entirely) before plunging himself into the lake.

Even after fifteen years, articles pertaining to Colin Firth, such as the Australian *Daily Telegraph*'s 'Don't Mention Mr Darcy' can't let go of Firth's associations with Darcy, the part that made the actor a household name: 'The faintest hint of a blush is visible under the whiskers he's still sporting after finishing another film shoot last week. I'd hoped the story might lead to a playful game of words, with Firth choosing between options such as film or stage, love or fight, and pride or prejudice. (The reasoning being that Firth – aka Mr Darcy – is probably sick to death of the standard promotional trail questions about that scene a decade ago when he emerged from a lake in those britches.) Except he doesn't seem too keen'.[15] Mary Colbert, in *The Sydney Morning Herald*, likewise begins her article 'Oh Mr Darcy', 'The unthinkable has happened: British actor Colin Firth is talking about "shagging". Mr Darcy, shagging?'[16] An article in *The*

[15] Fiona Hudson, *The Daily Telegraph* (Australia), 13/01/06, http://www.firth.com/articles/06dailytelau_113.html. Accessed 05/02/10.

Daily Express in 2007 kicks off with 'Colin Firth's image as Mr Darcy has clung to him tighter than the wet shirt he so famously wore when he emerged from a lake in *Pride And Prejudice*. But it's time, he says, to confess some home truths. He's just a kid from the local comprehensive who got lucky.'[17] In fact, it's difficult to find any review of Firth's later films without the seemingly obligatory reference to Mr Darcy.

The cost of the series was estimated at six million pounds.[18] Compared to the 29 million spent on Joe Wright's 2005 film, this was an exceptional bargain, with videos and DVDs continuing to be released into the 21st century. It even inspired a BBC advert featuring Mr Darcy returning to Pemberley, unexpected and dripping wet, with the explanation that he returned early because he needed to pay the BBC licence fee. Virtually every Austen adaptation since this has entered into some sort of comparison with this *Pride and Prejudice*, with the 1995 adaptation invariably coming out on top. Joe Wright's adaptation was beset with such comparisons and the reviews of this film continue to tell us as much about its predecessor. Peter Bradshaw in *The Guardian* writes: 'This new adaptation may not find favour everywhere, and it is not obviously daring or revisionist in the Andrew Davies manner; there is nothing to remind you of the classic *Punch* cartoon about Jane Austen's shocked editor telling her to take out all the effing and blinding.'[19] As Derek Elley predicts in *Variety*, 'Aficionados of the

[16] Mary Colbert, *The Sydney Morning Herald*, 05/05/06, http://www.firth.com/articles/06smh_505.html. Accessed 05/02/10.

[17] Garth Pearce, *Daily Express*, 29/09/07 http://www.firth.com/articles/07express_929.html. Accessed 05/02/10.

[18] Birtwistle, p. 27.

[19] Peter Bradshaw, *The Guardian*, http://www.guardian.co.uk/culture/2005/sep/16/2, accessed 26/01/10.

1995 five-hour BBC mini-series, with Jennifer Ehle as Elizabeth Bennet and Colin Firth as Mr Darcy won't necessarily be convinced by this big-screen version. But anyone coming to the movie fresh and not demanding a chapter-by-chapter adaptation will respond to the pic's emotional sweep, sumptuous lensing and marvelous sense of ensemble.'[20] Similarly, Peter Travers writing in *Rolling Stone* equally feels obliged to preface his review with a homage to the 1995 adaptation: 'granted that the peak is still the five-hour 1995 BBC mini-series starring Jennifer Ehle and a never-better Colin Firth. But even the most rabid Janeites must allow that director Joe Wright, 33, has given Austen's novel a beguilingly youthful spin without compromising the novel's late-eighteenth-century manners.'[21] In short, even in the face of competition, this adaptation has earned the overused classification, 'iconic', and for Colin Firth, the shadow of Mr Darcy has become, intentionally or unintentionally, a part of every role he's played since. To list a single example, the *mise en scène* in *St Trinians* (2007), when after falling in the water, Firth's character approaches the head mistress in wet shirt, is an unmistakable copy of the wet-shirted Darcy of 1995. The 1995 series in some respects has usurped the original in the minds of many fans, often shocked to discover that the lake sequence is not in the novel.

[20] Derek Elley, *Variety*, 11/09/05, http://www.variety.com/review/VE1117928133.html?categoryid=31&cs=1&p=0, accessed 26/01/10.

[21] Peter Travers, *Rolling Stone*, 03/11/05, http://www.rollingstone.com/reviews/movie/8748997/review/8749101/pride_and_ prejudice, accessed 26/01/10.

Picturing the past and 'the charm of recollection': cinematic adaptations of *pride and prejudice*, 1940, 2005

Austen's attribution of Mrs Gardiner's pleasure in Derbyshire to 'the charm of recollection' is an apt account of the appeal of cinematic reproductions of *Pride and Prejudice,* increasingly characterised by a range of intertextual references to other adaptations. But for some critics (especially early ones) the delights of intertextuality are the disappointments encountered by imposing economically driven formulae upon a well known story, articulated by Margaret Kennedy in *The Mechanized Muse* (1942), a book in which the author laments what she perceives as Hollywood's replacement of authors with machines. For Kennedy, if Jane Austen were a screenwriter she would simply be asked to supply a stock story: 'Jane Austen had she lived to-day, might have been asked to supply the "story" of *Pride and Prejudice* without any of the characterization, any of the idiomatic touches which lie in her dialogue. *Mr Collins proposes to Elizabeth* would have been thought sufficient.'[1]

[1] Margaret Kennedy, *The Mechanized Muse* (London: George Allen & Unwin, 1942), p. 25.

Published two years after the first film adaptation of the book, it seems a logical deduction that Kennedy had Robert Z. Leonard's *Pride and Prejudice* in mind when making these comments, but her judgement about the formulaic or mechanised method of novel adaptation seems harsh when applied to this film. The pressbook identifies the film as a 'picturization of Jane Austen's widely read novel'[2] and starring Greer Garson and Laurence Olivier (based on the theatrical adaptation by Helen Jerome), it is a far remove from adaptations that follow. Looking at it now, Darcy and Elizabeth appear far too old (Garson was 35 or 36, Olivier, slightly younger) and Garson's Elizabeth, because of her age, in hindsight, comes across as irritatingly culpable for her unbecoming idleness and studied coquettish behaviour. Significantly, as far as we know, it's the first film adaptation of a Jane Austen novel. The Helen Jerome play, published in 1936,[3] lends some theatrical touches to the film but the play is a much more simplified version of the novel, with three sisters rather than five and with a dilution of the novel's romantic complexities. In the play, Wickham chooses Lydia first, Collins has Elizabeth as his first choice of wife, and Jane becomes a version of Marianne in *Sense and Sensibility*, a victim of love-sickness; but unlike Marianne, rescued by Bingley, she is granted her first choice of husband. Elizabeth's intelligence, arrogance and bookishness are constantly highlighted in Jerome's adaptation and she utterly deserves her come-uppance at the play's close, blaming her pride for her bad behaviour. Her self-revelation is corrected by Darcy:

[2] 'The Career of Laurence Olivier'. *Pride and Prejudice*, Pressbook, 1940.

[3] Helen Jerome, *Pride and Prejudice Dramatized from Jane Austen's Novel* (London and Manchester: Samuel French Limited, 1936).

Elizabeth (*sits*). I am so ashamed!

(*Her head is down. A tear glistens on her cheek; the sight fills him with tenderness.*)

If you had not been noble and just you would have hated me. (*She shakes her head.*) I was the stupid one . . . the foolishly proud one.

Darcy (*tenderly*). No my dearest . . . only the prejudiced one . . .[4]

In this version, Elizabeth is both proud and prejudiced.

The 1940 film was inspired by a visit to a 1935 performance of the play by Harpo Marx, with plans for the casting of Clark Gable and Norma Shearer. The project was shelved until 1939 and was produced under very different conditions. As Ellen Belton has described, Karen Morley, the actress who played Charlotte Lucas, recalled the 'disturbing effect on the actors of the unfolding news of Hitler's march through the Netherlands and Belgium during the filming'.[5] It's tempting to read the adaptation as a nostalgic tribute to the Edenic England that is worth fighting for during the war years. The changes made to the narrative in the film – in particular, Mr Collins's change of profession from clergyman to opportunistic librarian (to placate the film's censors), the excision of the visit to Pemberley and Lady Catherine's test of Elizabeth's worthiness, to ensure that Elizabeth is marrying Darcy for love not money, are

---

[4] Ibid., p. 80.

[5] Ellen Belton, 'Reimagining Jane Austen: the 1940 and 1995 film versions of *Pride and Prejudice*', *Jane Austen on Screen*, eds Gina MacDonald and Andrew F. MacDonald (Cambridge: Cambridge University Press, 2003), p. 178.

worth unpacking in light of the war-time context. While the reason given for the transformation of Lady Catherine from vulgar snob to sweet old lady is that the actress playing her, Edna May Oliver, refused to play a villain, this rewriting of the story about the need to marry out of love not money may have been inserted to soften the perception of Britain for a US audience, in anticipation of an American alliance with Britain in the Second World War.[6] Significant for its omission is the visit to Pemberley. In 1940, the cost of the set is possibly a factor in its omission but so too is the need to paint a positive picture of the British for Americans on the verge of joining forces in the war. Censoring any mention of Elizabeth's potential materialism ('to be mistress of Pemberley might be something!') makes the heroine unequivocally an idealist rather than realist, bent on love rather than money. The film rewrites the novel to expose the hypocrisy of the British class system, democratising Darcy in his gradual conversion by Elizabeth to accepting a more equal society. Darcy's overheard rebuke of Elizabeth, for instance, is revised from, 'She is tolerable; but not handsome enough to tempt *me* and I am of no humour at present to give consequence to young ladies who are slighted by other men' (9), to 'A provincial young lady with a lively wit! Heaven preserve it. She looks tolerable enough, but I'm in no humour tonight to give consequence to the middle classes at play'. The 'Americanisation' and the idealisation of the British seem to have worked as a tonic to a war-torn audience, as Betty Howard's thank you letter to the director in 1941 suggests:

My husband is a Naval Officer and a few days ago he had one of his rare afternoons in port and a chance to visit the cinema.

---

[6] Liora Brosh, *Screening Novel Women: Gender in the British Nineteenth Century Novel and its Film Adaptations* (Houndmills: Palgrave, 2008), p. 19.

> We went to see your film made from the book we know and love
> so well and to our delight were carried away for two whole hours
> of perfect enjoyment. Only once was I reminded of our war –
> when in a candle-lit room there was an uncurtained window
> and my husband whispered humorously, 'Look – they're not
> blacked out.'[7]

The film focuses on the breakdown of class barriers and the consumerism and advancement of the middle classes. Significantly, it opens with the girls shopping, a possible clue to their upward mobility. Similarly, Lydia's transgression is seen as economic as well as sexual; her desire is not just to have a lover, but to have the physical accoutrements of marriage, such as carriages and liveries.[8] Typical of films of the 30s and 40s, the movie asks us to look at the costumes (anachronistic lavish hoop skirt designs) rather than through them[9] and even for a period drama, as Christine Geraghty observers, the costumes are excessive in the extreme and seem to function to 'endlessly distract from the narrative in order to please the eye':[10]

> So, after the crisis between Elizabeth and Darcy during the party
> at Netherfield, the next scene begins with Elizabeth watering a
> window box in what appears to be a tailored dress. The dark

 [7] Quoted in Kenneth Turan, '*Pride and Prejudice*: An Informal History of the Garson-Olivier Motion Picture', *Persuasions*, 11 (1989), pp. 140–43, http://www.jasna.org/persuasions/printed/number11/turan.htm. Accessed 08/05/10.

[8] Brosh, pp. 30–1.

[9] See Stella Bruzzi, *Undressing Cinema: Clothing and Identity in the Movies* (London: Routledge, 1997).

[10] Christine Geraghty, *Now a Major Motion Picture: Film Adaptation of Literature and Drama* (Rowman & Littlefield, 2008), p. 36.

color might be deemed to reflect her mood, but this interpretation is undermined by her deliberate pose and the
extravagance of the costume. The camera moves out to reveal
huge sleeves, dramatically slashed in black and white, with
contrasting cuffs and a matching striped skirt and then shows
Jane and Charlotte, equally elaborately dressed, attending to a
group of puppies.[11]

The film is marketed as a comedy at the expense of the women,
with the famous opening line of the novel translated in the adverts
as 'Bachelors Beware' and 'FIVE LOVE HUNGRY BEAUTIES IN SEARCH
OF HUSBANDS'. The women are visually ridiculous in their unmistake-
ably antebellum, *Gone with the Wind*-style costumes (undoubtedly
cashing in on the previous year's blockbuster film), especially when
the Bennet women fill the rooms to capacity, to the great risk of the
furniture, resembling a flock of squawking birds. The pressbook
expresses considerable pride in the accuracy of the costumes,
boasting that the Metro-Goldwyn-Mayer Research Department
consulted *Ackermann's Repository of Art and Fashion*, 40 volumes
outlining English fashion, furnishing, and architecture from 1809 to
1829. Claims to accuracy are undermined by the sweeping
statements about the novel in the pressbook, erroneously referring
to Elizabeth as the eldest of the five sisters. At a time where the
young male population was at risk, the women can be seen here
to be threatening in their domination, appropriating the role of the
male suitor in their outspoken quest for a partner, no more apparent
than in the carriage race between the Lucas and Bennet women,
each party determined to be the first to secure Mr Bingley's
acquaintance. However, Elizabeth is distinguished from the others

[11] Ibid., pp. 36–7.

in that she appears more knowing than her siblings in her awareness of their ridiculousness to others; she's often seen gazing out of a window, a reflection of both her objectification by the camera (framing her as in a painting) and her transitional status between inside her parental home and outside in the marriage market, between being a daughter and a wife. The framing of Elizabeth, on one level, objectifies her and can be regarded as scopophilic, as famously defined by Laura Mulvey, the object of the camera's male gaze.[12] But the framing also draws an analogy between adaptation and painting.

While the film commences with us looking at Elizabeth as if she's a figure in a painting, by the end of the movie she is pictured from behind looking out of the window, like Rapunzel waiting for her knight in shining armour to rescue her from her prison house. The film subtly moves from picturing the women as dominant and confident to solitary and vulnerable, as the film implies these women – like the country they inhabit – aren't really capable of coping on their own. Given the period in which it was produced, the representation of the English landscape would touch a chord. The view of Lady Catherine's Rosings, for instance, has all the hallmarks of a 19th century painting. Importantly, we gaze at the house through the eyes of Elizabeth. The *mise en scène* draws our eye on a diagonal axis, from the poultry at the bottom of the frame to the servant tending the garden, to the carriage of the aristocracy, to the great house on the top of the hill. The past is painted for us, like a 19th century painting, such as Constable's 'Admiral's House' (1820–23), with a visual layering of classes working together in perfect harmony.

The screenplay was co-written by Aldous Huxley, widely known as a novelist and journalist, an interesting choice of writer, given his

[12] Laura Mulvey, 'Visual Pleasure and Narrative Cinema', *Screen* 16 (3), pp. 6–18.

early attack on adaptations in 'the feelies' in his best known novel, *Brave New World* (1932) and in his published assault on the talkies in his earlier journalism. On the subject of the introduction of sound in *The Jazz Singer* (1929), Huxley writes, 'I felt ashamed of myself for listening to such things', savagely reflecting that the words will be regarded as 'worthy of the pen of a Racine or Dryden'.[13] Seemingly undergoing a complete *volte-face*, he settled in California, making a living as a screenwriter. His co-writer, Jane Murfin, is probably the major influence on the script with Huxley's name being used to signify the quality of the words and respect for the novel. Huxley is reported to have felt extremely guilty for the amount of money he received in Hollywood; this is either due to his shame in the final product or his lack of involvement in the writing.[14] No doubt, with the help of Huxley's name, the film was marketed as 'authentic' Austen. The focus in this adaptation is on the women, they dominate virtually every frame and indeed are 'pictured' by the camera as objects to look at.

Surprisingly another 'straight' feature film doesn't come along for 65 years, perhaps due to the dominance and popularity of television adaptations. This time, rather than positioning the women to be looked at, we look through them, or more particularly through the point of view of Elizabeth Bennet. Joe Wright's recent film, typical of postmodern adaptations, is as much reliant on previous film and television versions of *Pride and Prejudice* as it is on Austen's novel. Darcy takes a secondary position to Keira Knightly, whose star status arguably reduces the character of Elizabeth to star

---

13 Aldous Huxley, 'Silence is Golden', *Authors on Film*, ed. Harry M. Geduld (Bloomington and London: Indiana University Press, 1972), p. 70, p. 72.

14 Virginia M. Clark, *Aldous Huxley on Film* (New Jersey and London: The Scarecrow Press, 1987), p. 41.

vehicle — Knightley's performance in the film certainly captured the public imagination and resulted in an Oscar nomination.

Screenwriter Deborah Moggach has admitted that her screenplay was doomed to be overshadowed by Andrew Davies' 1995 version and responded to this pressure by setting the film in the earlier period, the late 18th century, at the time in which the novel was first drafted (opposed to the time of its publication in the early 19th century). Marketed through what Austen herself calls 'the charm of recollection', the poster of the film, picturing Kiera Knightley in profile looking to her right, is visually reminiscent of Ang Lee's *Sense and Sensibility* (1996) with Emma Thompson as Elinor in the same position, both women wearing earthy brown garments, with shades of yellow and green in the background; the implication is that if you liked *Sense and Sensibility*, you'll like this too.[15] Once again, film takes liberties which would be unheard of in television adaptation, prompting critics like Lisa Hopkins to rage against the butchering of Austen's prose:

At times indeed it sounds as though the dialogue has been mistranscribed by someone who simply failed to grasp the subtlety and nuances of either Austen's syntax or her humour: Elizabeth says of Bingley 'and conveniently rich'; Mr Collins says 'Before I am run away with my feelings', which is simply garbled (he means 'run away with *by* my feelings'), as are Mr Bennet's advice to Lizzie to choose Wickham to jilt her because 'He's a pleasant fellow and he'd do the job credibly' (he means 'creditably') and Mr Darcy's question 'Do you talk as a rule while dancing?'. All of these instances are objectionable not on the naïve grounds of infidelity but because they evince an insensitivity to the rules of English syntax, the keyboard on which Austen demonstrates her virtuoso technique.[16]

Similarly, Carol M. Doyle, reacts to the film's many 'infidelities', including Lady Catherine's bizarrely timed visit to the Bennets in the middle of the night, and misguided attempts at realism, especially in the film's obsession with mud.[17] However, in what she calls, 'the muddy hem version', Moggach wanted to emphasise the Bennets' poverty and the real sense of destitution and dependence haunting all the sisters. In contrast to the 1940 film, Christine Geraghty notes how the costumes in this film are deliberately worn looking and much more comfortable in appearance, with Elizabeth almost always in earthy colours, reflecting her naturalness and lack of ostentation.[18] The film is written entirely from Elizabeth's point of view, made apparent in the opening sequence in which a steadicam shot literally follows Elizabeth into and through Longbourn. In contrast to Leonard's Elizabeth, who is frequently pictured looking out of a window, this Elizabeth is initially seen looking in from the outside, culminating in her, towards the end, looking disdainfully at the newly married Wickham and Lydia from inside gazing out.

Even when she's not present, we see from her point of view, as in the scene in which Netherfield is being closed down through the sequence in which the wigged servants drape white sheets over all of the furniture, symbolising the shrouding of the place and the death knell to the hopes of the young girls, so reliant on the life of that place for their future happiness. Here is an occasion where the

[16] Lisa Hopkins, *Relocating Shakespeare and Austen on Screen* (Houndmills: Palgrave, 2009), p.149.

[17] Doyle, p. 5–10, http://www.jasna.org/persuasions/on-line/vol27no2/dole.htm

[18] Geraghty, *Now a Major Motion Picture*, pp. 88–9.

screenwriter, knowingly or not, uses another Austen adaptation as a source. In this case it's an adaption of *Persuasion* (Dear/Michell, 1995), in which as Katherine Sutherland relates, the direction reads: 'The linen billows around Anne. It's a sad picture, as if the deceased house is being wrapped in a shroud. On and on it goes: an ocean of white linen.'[19] Particularly striking in the 2005 adaptation is Mr Collins's proposal sequence. As Moggach has noted, Elizabeth is deserted, one by one by her family, like a lamb to its slaughter. Her father is the last to, knowingly, turn his back on Elizabeth and the sense of abandonment is keenly expressed in the horror on Elizabeth's face. After the refusal is announced to mothers and sisters, the camera fleetingly pauses on Mary's wistful expression, to suggest that she would have issued a 'yes' in Elzabeth's place. On hearing the news, Donald Sutherland's Mr Bennet soberly delivers the lines to Elizabeth, 'I will never see you again if you do' (marry Collins). The close-up on Sutherland, with his back to the women, shows a face momentarily full of despair, as if the final opportunity of saving his family has been sacrificed for the love of his daughter. In this way, Wright, almost imperceptibly, inserts back stories for the other characters in the film, so that we avoid accepting them at face value alone. Even Mary has her own story.

The emotion of the characters is clearly more apparent than in the 1940 adaptation and the costumes similarly function in this version to be looked through rather than to be looked at. In addition to the lovers' reunion at dawn, with Darcy in an open shirt reminiscent of Colin Firth's 1995 dripping Darcy, Elizabeth's costumes function to reveal rather than conceal the shape of the actress, most obviously in the first proposal sequence, set in a folly outside Rosings in the pouring rain.

---

[19] Quoted in Sutherland, p. 346.

Elizabeth's unacknowledged attraction to Darcy is clear when he first helps her into the carriage outside Netherfield; he holds onto her hand for slightly longer than absolutely necessary and this first touch, in which a close-up of the hands detaches them from their bodies, clearly registers on Elizabeth's face in the next shot and anticipates their final pairing in which Elizabeth quite literally accepts his hands by taking them into her own, uttering, 'Your hands are cold'. As I discussed in 'A timeline of *Pride and Prejudice* adaptations', pp. 3–24, Wright employs a well-known cinematic code in the dance sequence at Netherfield; the shot of the crowded dance floor glides into a shot of Darcy and Elizabeth, suddenly dancing alone in the room. Similarly, during the visit to Pemberley, Elizabeth's aunt and uncle seem to vanish, leaving Elizabeth alone to confront Darcy and to make her own way back to Lambton. Wright pours on the romantic with both lower and upper case 'r's.[20] Before the trip to Derbyshire Mary utters the romantic aphorism (spoken by Elizabeth in the novel), 'What are men compared to rocks and mountains', echoed by Mr Gardiner just before the tourists arrive at Pemberley.[21] The external shots of Derbyshire, in particular the helicopter shot of Elizabeth positioned precariously on the precipice of a craggy rock taking in the spectacular view with the wind blowing through her garments, invites comparison with a score of Romantic paintings, often chosen as covers for collections of Romantic poetry, such as John Casper Friederick's 'The Wanderer' (1818) or Henry Fuseli's 'The Ladies of

---

[20] For the influence of Romanticism on Joe Wright's film, see Sarah Ailwood, 'What are men to rocks and mountains?': Romanticism in Joe Wright's *Pride & Prejudice, Persuasions On-line*, 27 (2), http://www.jasna.org/persuasions/on-line/vol27no2/ailwood.htm. Accessed 10/05/10.

[21] In the novel, it is 'What are men to rocks and mountains' (103).

Hastings' (1798–1800), in which lonely windswept figures are juxtaposed with dramatically expansive landscapes in which spectacular skies threaten an imminent storm. Like the 1940 film, the pictures, call attention to the work as an adaptation *qua* adaptation (insofar as we're made aware that the film is based on art), but the English landscapes here, rather than being presented as something worthy of defending as in the Leonard film, are revealed more as appealing places to visit, reminiscent of advertisements for the British Tourist Board. These enticing vistas remind us of what Mike Crang identifies as Austen's contribution to 'literary tourism'.[22] Following the novel, the adaptation not only describes tourism but inspires it as well, to mention just one example, a visit to Burghley House (the site for Rosings) will include a viewing of some of the more lavish costumes of this particular version of *Pride and Prejudice*.

The film oscillates between these Romantic exteriors, Vermeer and Hogarth-inspired interiors (for instance Hogarth is recalled in the picture of the Bennets, complete with dog, hunched over their heaped breakfast table), to increasingly mouth-watering country houses: Basildon Park, Berkshire (Netherfield), Burghley House, Stamford (Rosings) and Chatsworth House (Pemberley); the latter often thought to be the inspiration for Darcy's estate, given that it's the most significant house of its kind in Derbyshire. In this version, instead of looking at a portrait of Darcy, Elizabeth finds Darcy's bust in the midst of a sculpture gallery, which simultaneously evokes erotic awakening, through the sexual posturing of the figures, and mourning; the place, as Deborah Moggach has observed, resembles a mausoleum. Dario Marianelli's music which accompanies Elizabeth into the house, at the opening of the film, where

[22] 'Placing Jane Austen, Displacing England: Touring between Book, History, and Nation', Pucci and Thompson, eds, pp. 111–30.

we discover the non-diegetic music is actually diegetic with Mary seen from behind playing the pianoforte is repeated in Elizabeth's wandering through Pemberley; this time the pianoforte player is Darcy's sister. The fact that the music is the same as that of the opening sequence intimates that Elizabeth has found another home in Pemberley. It also calls attention to the magnetic appeal of the pianoforte, as a feature of Austen and in adaptations of her novels, in general.[23] Elizabeth is awakened to the reality that she is an interloper, not one of the family, when she is caught eavesdropping on Georgiana by Darcy, and the couple's awkward meeting is kept brief, possibly so as not to enter competition with the famous 1995 rendition of this chapter. Nonetheless, Elizabeth's behaviour is hard to fathom: she runs away, like Cinderella frightened of her coach turning into a pumpkin, and finds herself mysteriously on her own, her aunt and uncle having inexplicably vanished, leaving her to face Darcy alone. The inevitable intertextual reference to the 1995 meeting of Darcy in a wet diaphanous shirt, as mentioned above, is postponed until the climax of the 2005 version, with Darcy and Elizabeth meeting at dawn, both restless after the visitation of Lady Catherine, and with Darcy in an open shirt and flowing overcoat, a clear nod to Firth's Darcy's famous state of undress.

Like the 1940 film, this production claims authenticity while breaking the illusion at the same time; while the fabrics and the interiors seem very much 'true' to the late 18th century, it is unlikely that a woman of this period could wander around so freely without a hat, or meet a suitor at dawn wearing a dressing gown. It's also unlikely that Mr Bennet would have Donald Sutherland's perfect teeth. Sutherland brings to this film his star status but is somewhat disruptive to the plausibility of the story given his age; at 70, he's far

[23] See 'A timeline of *Pride and Prejudice* adaptations', pp. 14–18.

too old to be Elizabeth's father and at near 50, at the time of his marriage, he should have been sufficiently experienced to see through the ephemeral charms of his future wife. The ages of Mr and Mrs Bennet are exaggerated in mainstream adaptations; married for 23 years, it's unlikely that Mrs Bennet, in particular, would be much above 40. Admittedly, 40 would look very different in the early 19th century than it does in the early 21st century, but Mrs Bennet's potential jealousy of Mr Bennet's favourite daughter could account for Elizabeth being 'the least dear' to Mrs Bennet of 'all her children' (71) reflected in the mother's unhesitating sacrifice of her daughter to Mr Collins. After all, the relationship between father and daughter is more of an equal partnership than that between husband and wife, the connotations of which are noticeably repressed in 21st century adaptations, such as the 2005 film and *Becoming Jane* in which the parents are seen in bed together, clearly very fond of each other's company; Elizabeth is in no way a rival to her mother, as she may be construed to be in Austen's novel.[24]

Although we can forgive the inevitable anachronisms, the 2005 film's final impression is marred by the 'alternative ending' in which a post-coital Elizabeth and Darcy discuss what Darcy should call Elizabeth, now that they are married: 'You may only call me Mrs Darcy when you are completely, perfectly, and incandescently happy'. While poor American audiences would be reaching for the sick bowl, British viewers were spared this ending and, on the whole, found this a very satisfying film adaptation, with Kiera Knightley, with her unusual features and believable youthfulness, a very convincing Elizabeth.

[24] For a discussion of the valorising of Mr Bennet in *Bride and Prejudice* and this film see, Barbara K. Seeber, 'A Bennet Utopia: Adapting the Father in *Pride and Prejudice*', *Persuasions On-line* 27 (2), 2007, http://www.jasna.org/persuasions/on-line/vol27no2/seeber.htm. Accessed 06/05/10.

Jane Austen's own 'picturization' (to borrow the term for adaptation used so prominently in 1940 pressbook) of her art is famously of a miniature on ivory and intriguingly within *Pride and Prejudice* it is the miniature of Darcy that captures Elizabeth's eye at Pemberley; Elizabeth never replies to Mrs Gardiner's question 'But, Lizzy, you can tell us whether it is like or not' (160). A qualitative assessment of the miniature is provocatively withheld from the reader and this picture is replaced in the narrative for a larger version in which Elizabeth initially glances at, then returns to it with an intensified regard. As I have noted, the return to the picture mirrors Elizabeth's own change of mind about Darcy, and reflects the significance attached to second impressions in the novel as a whole. Austen, in a novel that as Tony Tanner has demonstrated, is full of pictures,[25] literally asks us to look at the larger picture, a complicated, perhaps impossible task for the reader of a declared miniaturist. Both film adaptations reflect upon themselves as pictures, both self-consciously framing their subject through the device of the window and offering the viewer pictures, inspired by famous paintings of the 19th century and, possibly, inspired by the pictures in the novel itself.

How far can we travel away from *Pride and Prejudice* before it becomes a completely different text? Austen's novel is omni-present in countless forms, and at times the presence is so shadowy as to become no longer eligible of the attribution of 'adaptation'.

---

[25] Tony Tanner, *Jane Austen* (Houndmills: Macmillan, 1986), pp. 116–120.

'The shades of pemberley to be thus polluted': loose adaptations

••

When Lady Catherine rudely asks Elizabeth 'Are the shades of Pemberley to be thus polluted?' through a Darcy/Bennet alliance, the answer for all readers is, of course, 'no'. And this can be said too, to the charge that adaptations contaminate Austen's novel, from the seemingly accurate to ones that are hardly recognisable as influenced by *Pride and Prejudice*. When we think of Austen adaptations, 'authentic' adaptations set in the Regency period immediately spring to mind. But as we have seen, no matter how much effort is put into the creation of authenticity, attempts to reconstruct the past ultimately reveal more about a film's present. Still it is the case that consistently, Austen adaptations that preserve some of the language of the novel, unlike Shakespeare films, on the whole are set in the time in which the novels were written.

However, those that abandon Austen's language, or modernisations of the work, are plentiful. If we go beyond the obvious adaptations of the story, including *Pride and Prejudice* (teenpic adaptation of 2003) *Bride and Prejudice* (Bollywood-style adaptation of 2004) and *Bridget Jones's Diary* (2001), we can find the story of *Pride and Prejudice* in a myriad of places. Recently, there have been adaptations, ranging from explicit to implicit borrowings from the novel and the list produced by my students and myself includes the following 'adaptations':

- *Lost In Austen*, 2008
- *Miss Austen Regrets*, 2008
- *Twilight*, 2008 (book: 2005)
- *Becoming Jane*, 2007
- *The Jane Austen Book Club*, 2007 (book: 2004)
- *Bridget Jones's Diary*, 2001 (book: 1996)
- *Sex and the City* TV series, 1998– (book: 1997)
- *You've Got Mail* (1998)
- *Pretty Woman* (1990)
- *When Harry Met Sally* (1989)
- Episode of *Dallas* entitled *Pride and Prejudice* (July 7, 1989)[1]
- *Beauty and the Beast* (1987)

No doubt many readers will dispute the inclusion of some of these as accidentally or incidentally close to Austen's narrative and many will have other texts to add to such a list. This section moves from loose to looser adaptations of the novel, and the survey itself inevitably poses the question about how far an adaptation can go before it ceases to be an adaptation. Shakespeare studies have embraced the presence of Shakespeare in popular culture, with a vast array of work ranging from studies of *The Lion King* and *Hamlet* to the *Klingon Shakespeare Restoration Project*.[2] In comparison,

---

[1] See p. 108 for an account of similarities between the series and *Pride and Prejudice*.

[2] See, for example, Douglas Lanier, *Shakespeare and Modern Popular Culture* (Oxford: Oxford University Press, 2002).

Austen scholarship, for most of the 20th century, has been relatively quiet on the subject of the novels in popular culture, in spite of the obvious influence of *Pride and Prejudice* on the genre of the popular romance novel and on romantic comedy.

Loose adaptations are, no doubt, no less 'unfaithful' than 'straight' versions and my conception of adaptations is in disagreement with Jocelyn Harris's contestation that 'Jane Austen versions cannot be considered faithful translations if the scriptwriters mangle her words, though some slips may be blamed on the carelessness of the actors'.[3] Indeed, it's of no consequence whether an adaptation is 'faithful' to Austen's words but it is clearly the case, the less they resemble the story as described by Austen, the less they are victims of the unfruitful 'not as good as the book' conclusions while being more prone to accusations of devaluing, dishonouring or trivialising Austen's narrative.

While undoubtedly supplying the basic narrative structure for the 'Harlequin' or mass-market romance novel, Austen herself has received the 'Harliquinisation' treatment in a number of 'heritage' and loose film adaptations. Harriet Margolis summarises how adaptations, like popular romance fiction based at least partially on Austen's novels, 'have been denigrated for failing to satisfy many of the evaluative criteria by which Austen's novels are academically judged successful. Romance novels are bad because they are mass-produced, formulaic, limited in scope, accepting of a patriarchal status quo, overly concerned with sex, almost exclusively concerned with heterosexual sex, and appealing only to an unintelligent readership, incapable of appreciating

[3] '"Such a Transformation": translation, imitation, and intertextuality in Jane Austen on screen', in MacDonald and MacDonald, eds, p. 48.

better writing'.[4] However, loose screen adaptations of Austen's novels – as has been demonstrated in the teenpic adaptation of *Emma*, *Clueless* (Amy Heckerling, 1995) – are often witty and knowing, self-consciously reflecting upon their status as adaptations; far from positing inferiority complexes, these adaptations often challenge Austen's representations from contemporary perspectives.

The 21st century begins with a flurry of takes on Jane Austen and her best known novel, *Pride and Prejudice*. The film *Bridget Jones's Diary* (2001) can be regarded, on one level, as an adaptation of an 'adaptation' of *Pride and Prejudice* by Helen Fielding (1996) – also an adaptation of the 1995 *Pride and Prejudice* – in which Elizabeth is transplanted to 1990s London, the caddish Wickham becomes Bridget's boss, Daniel Cleaver (played by Hugh Grant), and Darcy is transformed into a successful lawyer, Mark Darcy (played by Colin Firth in an undisguised revival of his role as Darcy in 1995). In a clever twist to Austen's narrative, rather than the youngest sister, Lydia, it is Bridget's mother who disgraces the family through her association with a criminal named Julio who embezzles several families' savings into non-existent timeshares. High-powered lawyer, Darcy, rescues the situation and becomes a textbook romantic hero at the close. Casting Colin Firth as Mark Darcy in the film (on, I am told, the recommendation of the screenwriter, Andrew Davies),[5] makes the connection between film and book/adaptation all the more explicit and as Lisa Hopkins notes, the film goes one stage further in alluding to Austen's novel by having Bridget overhear Mark abusing her at the Turkey Curry Buffet, a clear echo to the defining moment

[4] Harriet Margolis, 'Janeite culture: what does the name "Jane Austen" authorize?' in MacDonald and MacDonald, eds, p. 24.

[5] Conversation with Andrew Davies (unpublished).

in *Pride and Prejudice* when Elizabeth overhears Darcy's reaction to Elizabeth: 'She is tolerable; but not handsome enough to tempt *me*, and I am in no humour at present to give consequence to young ladies who are slighted by other men' (9). Darcy's 20th century counterpart is even more devastating in his first reaction to Bridget: 'Mother, I do not need a blind date. Particularly not with some verbally incontinent spinster . . . who smokes like a chimney, drinks like a fish . . . and dresses like her mother'.[6] Elizabeth is updated into Bridget, according to Shelley Cobb, through a post feminist lens,[7] in which the heroine feels, if possible, even more intently the cruelty of Darcy's words, making more explicit the penetrating consequence the words have on Bridget's life, being also the catalyst for the diary – and novel and film – itself.

Bridget's independence and single lifestyle are undermined by her frantic quest for a permanent boyfriend, ironically reflected in her favourite TV programmes, *Blind Date* and Andrew Davies' adaptation of *Pride and Prejudice* (in the film adaptation her dream becomes real with Colin Firth uniting Fitzwilliam Darcy and Mark Darcy). In the novel, the Assembly ball sequence is replaced by a book launch (hosted by Bridget's employer, Pemberley Press) in which the subject of conversation is ironically whether adaptations should be watched as replacement or without knowledge of their literary sources. Bridget's line manager, Perpetua, the Caroline Bingley figure, believes they should be banned while Bridget mischievously champions the popular over the classic.

[6] *Bridget Jones's Diary* script-dialogue transcript, http://www.script-o-rama.com/movie_scripts/b/bridget-jones-diary-script-transcript.html. Accessed 9/11/09.

[7] Shelley Cobb, 'Adaptable Bridget: Generic Intertextuality and Postfeminism in *Bridget Jones's Diary*, *Authorship in Film Adaptaion*, ed. Jack Boozer (Austin: University of Texas Press, 2008), pp. 281–304.

'And you do realize *Middlemarch* was originally a book, Bridget, don't you, not a soap?' . . .

'We were just talking about hierarchies of culture,' boomed Perpetua. 'Bridget is one of these people who thinks the moment when the screen goes back on *Blind Date* is on a par with Othello's 'hurl my soul from heaven' soliloquy,' she said, hooting with laughter.

'Ah. Then Bridget is clearly a top postmodernist,' said Mark Darcy.[8]

Of course, *Bridget Jones's Diary* can be regarded either as an adaptation of *Pride and Prejudice* or as a novel – or indeed, film – in its own right, without requiring any knowledge of Austen. It's worth noting, how, as Imelda Whelehan comments, the film accentuates the romantic by 'Harlequenising' the story: 'the fact that Darcy and Bridget's final encounter takes place in another strangely deserted street reminds us that all romances in formula fiction occur in a vacuum where work and the other petty commitments of life temporarily fall away.'[9] This is something that couldn't be said about *Pride and Prejudice*.

The subject of to adapt or not to adapt emerges in another take on Austen's novels, Karen Joy Fowler's *The Jane Austen Book Club* (2004), adapted into a film in 2007; this time the subject is Christina Rozema's 1999 film adaptation of *Mansfield Park*.

They talked more as they threaded through the seats. Jocelyn turned out to like fiddling about with the original story no better than Prudie did. The great thing about books was the solidity of

[8] Helen Fielding, *Bridget Jones's Diary* (London: Picador, 1997), pp. 100–101.
[9] *Helen Fielding's Bridget Jones's Diary* (New York: Continuum, 2002), p. 80.

the written word. You might change and your reading might change as a result, but the book remained whatever it had always been. A good book was surprising the first time through, less so the second.[10]

Once again the unhappy mixture of the classic with the popular provokes heated discussion with the only male member of the group averring that Austen's novels contribute much to the sit-com genre in which it is the minor characters who sustain the uniqueness and interest in the programmes in what are otherwise formulaic and mindless, aimed at the mass market.

It is the male character, Brigg, who if anyone, emerges as the Elizabeth figure, finding his Mr Darcy in the older woman Jocelyn, who shares his love of dogs, and who is initially disdainful of his popular tastes. This novel – an adaptation of all of Austen's published novels – makes clear that adaptations are 'readings' of the books, with the narrative of each book club meeting being an adaptation of the novel under discussion. And, as in *Bridget Jones's Diary* looser or radical adaptations, while applauded by the authors insofar as their novels are themselves examples of the genre, ironically receive opposition from the novel's protagonists, who consider any deviation from Austen's beloved novels as verging on blasphemy. The novel, albeit probably unwittingly, enacts a debate that has dogged the field of adaptation studies for most of the 20th century: to adapt or not to adapt, or whether it is nobler to change an author's words and 'intentions' or to abandon the quest altogether.

[10] Karen Fowler, *The Jane Austen Book Club* (London, New York, Toronto: Penguin, 2004), p. 82.

Certainly, for many, Andrew Black's *Pride & Prejudice* (2003), a Mormon teenpic adaptation, would have been better if it had never been made at all. The Mormon context serves to retain the importance Austen attaches to marriage, with Wickham (in my viewing, the most attractive character in the film), in the end being arrested in a seedy Las Vegas chapel with a very disappointed Lydia, replete in wedding dress, for three counts of bigamy and nine counts of illegal gambling. Austen's novel is recalled in the many books in the film, from Lydia's beloved *Pink Bible* (everything you need to know about dating), to Elizabeth's own novel which is the means of bringing her together with Darcy (who turns out to own the publishing company). Intertitles taken from *Pride and Prejudice*, with pastel backgrounds, punctuate the film, and the adaptation concludes with Elizabeth in England admiring the famous portrait of the novelist, with Darcy lovingly looking on. It's tempting to interpret Charles Bingley's business venture, 'Classics for Canines' in which he sells CDs of classical music for the consumption of dogs, presumably to make them smarter, as a parallel enterprise to the movie itself; although it's hard to imagine how Black could sell his film through belittling and insulting his audience, even covertly.

The DVD also has a 'pop-up' feature enabling 'references to Jane Austen's classic novel, *Pride & Prejudice*, to pop-up on your screen as you watch the movie'. A few minutes into the film, for instance, we see Elizabeth's professor in front of a blackboard laden with facts about Jane Austen and the pink pop-up explains 'Elizabeth is learning about Jane Austen and the lives of women in Regency England. The lecture is entitled "Rational Creature vs. Elegant Lady"'. When Elizabeth asks the girls to celebrate her invitation to meet a publisher, Lydia's excuse is she's meeting 'Denny and Carter, or is it Carter and Denny', while the pop-up reads, 'In the novel, Lydia and Kitty flirt with Captain Carter and Mr Denny, members of the shire militia'. While driving to church the girls are seen listening to the radio and the pink pop-up informs us that the 'radio station 181.3 The Juice is a reference to the year of *Pride and Prejudice*'s publication, 1813. Austen wrote the original draft of the novel in 1796/1797 under the title "First Impressions"'. Allusions to the author and novel are somewhat forced in both the adaptation and in its paratextual materials and seem to be invoked in order to repeatedly remind the viewer that this is an adaptation, as in this contemporary reconstruction of *Pride and Prejudice*, it's very easy to forget.

Another adaptation that stands on its own, not requiring previous knowledge of Austen, is *Bride and Prejudice* (2004), a Bollywood rewriting of the story within an Indian context, stunningly shot in Amritsar, Punjab, India, among other places. The Bollywood tradition, in which the hero and heroine never kiss, pleasingly accords with the decorous romances of Austen's novel. Gurinder Chadha's relinquishment of 'Pride' calls attention to the retained 'Prejudice' in the film's title, focussing on a more serious side of the story and one that effortlessly adapts to the 21st century. As the director's commentary makes clear, this is a film about a clash of cultures rather than about class confrontation and stars Bollywood star and ex-Miss World, Aishwarya Rai. Chadha and co-writer Paul Mayeda Berges play down any controversies inspired by the inter-racial relationship of the central pair, insisting that this would not be an issue in India. Nonetheless, the film seeks to put a positive spin on arranged marriages of convenience, as the DVD commentary states, the marriage between Mr Collins and Mrs Collins (the Kohlis) is explicitly a happy one, ultimately we are made to feel that they are genuinely in love. The cultural clash between India and the United States is dramatised through the central characters,

American Will Darcy with Indian, Lalita Bakhi. The film works on several levels, as director Gurinder Chadha remarks on the DVD commentary, the film draws on Bollywood traditions, such as the opening referencing a religious icon for good luck, with a shot of the Golden Temple.

Instead of playing the piano badly (or boringly), Maya, the Mary character, dances for the family in a tacky and cringe making routine that threatens to never end; a dance that, as the director indicates, is in a Bollywood tradition, adding another level to a knowing audience. Similarly, the fight between Darcy and Wickham in front of a Bollywood film, *Purab Aur Pachhim* (1970), one of the first Bollywood films about Indians in the UK, at the British Film Institute in London, according to Gurinder Chadha, references the origins of the movie in Bollywood cinema, but also is reminiscent of the fight between Mark Darcy and Daniel Cleaver in *Bridget Jones's Diary*. Almost imperceptible in the film is *Pride and Prejudice* itself, the novel that Lalita is reading on the beach with Darcy and Kiran, the Caroline Bingley figure. The presence of the book is a consistent feature of postmodern adaptations of *Pride and Prejudice* that, as we will see in the next section, makes Elizabeth, both like the author, in control of her story, and like the audience, the reader of her story. The film reveals its own origins in earlier films as well as in the novel when Mr Bakshi quotes Mr Bennet (from the 1940 film, a line not in the novel) in response to his wife's wailing that their four daughters are unmarried: 'perhaps we should have drowned one or two at the time of their birth'.[11]

Following from the discussion of how Austen seems to follow Shakespeare ('The novel and its reputation', pp. 25–45), her screen

[11] Noted by Barbara K. Seeber, 'A Bennet Utopia: Adapting the Father in *Pride and Prejudice*', *Persuasions On-line* 27 (2), 2007, http://www.jasna.org/persuasions/on-line/vol27no2/seeber.htm. Accessed 06/05/10.

history, likewise follows in the dramatist's footsteps. While Shakespeare had his TV time travelling episode in BBC's *Doctor Who* (*The Shakespeare Code*, 2007), Jane Austen gets hers in *Lost in Austen*, released in 2008 (ITV). The series is, in part, an adaptation of Emma Campbell Webster's interactive book in which readers' answers to questions dictates the page they turn to, *Lost in Austen: Choose Your Own Jane Austen Adventure*.[12] The game-inspired book is advertised on its frontispiece with:

> Ever wanted to travel around inside an Austen novel and wonder how you'd fare meeting Darcy for the first time? Think you could be smart enough to see through Wickham's little game? Emma Campbell Webster's ingenious guide to Jane's books will give YOU the chance to find out and is both amusing, enlightening, and un-Austen-tatious – a must-read for Jane Austen fans everywhere![13]

Lost in Austen, the four-part television series, features a time travel story involving an exchange between Elizabeth Bennet and her 21st century fan, bank clerk, Amanda Price, played by Jemima Rooper. Elizabeth slides almost effortlessly into the 21st century while the annoying Amanda has more difficulty adapting to manners, clothes, and sanitation of the late 18th century. The series poses some interesting questions about the contemporary fascination with Austen adaptations and adaptation in general, and the 21st century nostalgia for the pre-feminist world that Austen's books seem to represent, with Amanda telling her mother that she longs

---

[12] *Lost in Austen: Choose Your Own Jane Austen Adventure* (New York: Berkley Publishing Group, 2007).

[13] Jasper Fforde, cover insert, 'Praise for *Lost in Austen: Create Your Own Jane Austen Adventure*'.

for the manners, courtesy, and language of Austen's men. But, like *Bridget Jones's Diary*, the adaptation is even more explicitly an adaptation of the 1995 television series than Austen's novel, with Elizabeth Bennet looking at pictures of her future husband, Colin Firth, on the internet and Amanda having 'a postmodern moment', asking Mr Darcy to re-enact Firth's Darcy's famous swim.

Lost in Austen prefaces each episode with a cardboard cut-out Amanda, referred to by Laurie Kaplan as 'a contemporary Generation-Y "Everygirl"'[14] holding an oversized *Pride and Prejudice* book which she throws away as the credits roll, revealing to the audience that what they are going to see is not in the book. In fact, by episode three, Amanda rips up the book and throws it into the lake, only to be scooped up by Mr Darcy himself. Looking always out of place, Amanda (with her distinctive 21st century straightened hair, although how she obtains straighteners in the early 19th century is impossible to fathom) is upstaged and outwitted by the subtlety and humour of Austen's characters, each taking their personality traits onto a different level. Lydia no longer foolishly stumbles into an impetuous alliance with Wickham but is manipulative and sexually aware from the start of the story. Bingley is reduced to a drunk, and Wickham, a loveable prankster who has been maligned by Darcy, self-consciously defines himself as someone on the edge of society. Hearing his side of the story of the relationship between Georgiana and himself in which Georgiana is the culprit transforms him into the unsung hero of this adaptation.[15]

---

[14] '*Lost in Austen* and the Generation-Y Janenites', *Persuasions*, 30 (2), 2010, p. 3. http://www.jasna.org/persuasions/printed/pers30.html. Accessed 06/05/10.

[15] Such a vindication of Wickham may be behind the figure of Robbie in Ian McEwan's *Atonement* who shares a number of Wickham's characteristics, being patronised by the landowners and wrongly accused of sexual violation and betrayal. Thanks to Ian Bradley for suggesting this to me.

Caroline Bingley – 'Frosty-knickers' to Amanda – is revealed to be a lesbian, Darcy a young man who clearly has too much time on his hands, and Mr Bennet, bewilderingly, takes Amanda in as his confidant, even revealing his previously undisclosed name – 'Claude'. Jane dutifully marries Collins and Mrs Bennet is unlike any of her previous incarnations in that her stupidity is replaced with malice. This is a very evil mother or as Amanda puts it, 'a ball breaker'. Thanks to Amanda, she and Jane are eventually transformed and are able to give Lady Catherine as good as she gives. The series was greeted with the typical Austen critical approach, reviewers forecasting that the audience will either love it or hate it and, like the majority of early 20th century lovers of the novels, the series' appeal through escapist charms are duly noted: 'It was just the thing to forget the economic crisis for a few hours and just enjoy watching television again. This is a romantic fantasy of the highest caliber. It is only right that such a series would come from British television'.[16] As mentioned, typical of postmodern adaptations, the series is more an adaptation of an adaptation and the selfishness and brazenness of the central character has more in common with Bridget Jones than Elizabeth Bennet (with the fight between Darcy and Amanda's boyfriend, Michael, in the final episode, clearly an intertextual reference to *Bridget Jones's Diary*). Indeed, in rejecting her laddish boyfriend, Michael, Amanda becomes his replica in Regency society (or a laddette version of him), imposing upon Darcy the very fate that she escaped from in the 21st century: a marriage of contrasting sensibilities.

Amanda, like many of Austen's critics, unknowingly belittles the novelist through reading *Pride and Prejudice* as a means of escape, with the lines, 'It is a truth generally acknowledged that

---

[16] Image Entertainment, http://www.hometheaterinfo.com/lost_in_austen.htm. Accessed 21/08/09.

we are all longing to escape. I escape always to my favourite book *Pride and Prejudice*. I've read it so many times now the words just say themselves in my head and it's like a window opening, it's like I'm actually there. It's become a place I know so intimately I can see that world, I can touch it. I can see Darcy. Whoa, Amanda.', but her experience in the story proves otherwise (perhaps most memorably when she receives twigs and chalk to clean her teeth – and the first thing Amanda does on returning to Hammersmith is to give her teeth a good clean). Elizabeth is hardly on camera and, in hindsight, her story of experiencing West End London, from a trip on the underground to a visit to Harrods, might be a more interesting story to tell. As she tells Amanda after booking a taxi with her credit card: she was 'born out of time and out of place'. Her views on television – she likes to look but not listen – call attention to the clash of languages that characterises the series (the reconstructed ornate sentence constructions of the late 18th century as contrasted with the crude expressions of the 21st). The jarring tones of Amanda's voice are visualised in the dancing sequence, where the elegant movement and banter of Austen's period is contrasted with her conversing and moving out of sequence. Nonetheless, the swapping of roles reveals Elizabeth as a woman of the future, Amanda as a woman of the past; while Elizabeth is admired for her modernity, Amanda's passion for the past is a fabricated one, based on modern re-readings, which as the series points out, carefully excise the darker sides of Austen's world, where the likelihood would be for Jane to marry Collins and Charlotte to opt for the life of a missionary in Africa in order to avoid a degrading life of dependent spinsterhood. But the series cannot go so far as to show Jane's marriage to a singularly odious Mr Collins consummated, allegedly too repulsive for a 21st century audience. Love it or hate it, *Lost in Austen* owes more to *Pride and*

Prejudice's adaptation history than to the novel itself, the costumes themselves recalling a host of other versions of Austen's story. To list a few, the tan Spencer Amanda wears for the journey to Hammersmith and the bonnet she wears at Longbourn were worn by Jennifer Ehle (Elizabeth Bennet) in *Pride and Prejudice* (1995) and the plaid Spencer worn by Gemma Arterton (Elizabeth Bennet) in Amanda's bathroom was worn by Susannah Harker (Jane Bennet) in the 1995 adaptation when she rode to Netherfield in the rain.[17] Rather than using costumes to be looked at (as in the 1940 *Pride and Prejudice*) or to look through (as in the 2005 adaptation), costume here functions to recall other adaptations, covertly inviting the viewer to contemplate the process of adaptation itself and, especially, how far it has come from fruitlessly maintaining the illusion of stemming from a single source text.

Much of this book has dwelt upon the significance of the novel's initial title, 'First Impressions' and the importance of second impressions, the need for reflection and impartiality and a warning of the consequences of impulsive, knee-jerk responses to characters and situations. Austen's concern is with re-evaluations, second readings (adaptations themselves), what has been identified by Stanley Cavell in *Pursuits of Happiness* as 'the Hollywood Comedy of Remarriage'.[18] These film narratives of second chances can be seen in a range of other novels, films, and television texts, such as *When Harry Met Sally* (1989), *You've Got Mail* (1998) or *Beauty and the Beast* (1991).

Whether it is deliberate or accidental, cinema's appropriation of literary texts is frequently concealed in the films' titles, testified

[17] http://www.imdb.com/title/tt1117666/trivia. Accessed 08/01/10.

[18] Stanley Cavell, *Pursuits of Happiness: The Hollywood Comedy of Remarriage* (Cambridge Mass: Harvard University Press, 1981).

by the examples above. Television programmes, on the other hand, often borrow literary titles and emulate their narratives, on one level, as a challenge to preconceived hierarchies of value in which TV is ranked culturally lowest. An example of these borrowings is the long running serial, *Dallas*, which increasingly veered to titles with literary or cinematic associations. To list just a few are *Paradise Lost*, *Decline and Fall*, *Fathers and Sons*, *A Tale of Two Cities*, *Phantom of the Oil Rig*, and, of course, *Pride and Prejudice*. This episode involved matriarch Miss Ellie and her second husband, Clayton in a search for a message left to Miss Ellie's first husband, Jock. Meanwhile her son, the wildly ambitious and unscrupulous J.R. is becoming increasing drawn to the son of an ex-flame, who we later discover, predictably, is J.R.'s biological child. While it's difficult to find traces of *Pride and Prejudice* in this particular episode, the series as a whole has a structure not that far removed from Austen's narrative: the strong relationship between J.R. and Sue Ellen which after numerous 'second chances' is finally cemented at the end and the triangular relationship of Lizzie, Wickham, and Darcy, possibly present in Dallas's back story, involving the triangular relationship between Miss Ellie, Jock Ewing, and Digger Barnes.

More alarm bells are raised through these loose adaptations about the differences rather than the similarities between novel and adaptation, such as the unintentional pleasure derived by observing Mr Darcy played by a Jack Russell dog in the cult children's series, *Wishbone* (1995–98), a series which based its episodes on the dog's re-enactments of literary classics. This may be the ultimate message of *Lost in Austen*: that we are struck by the mis-fit of Amanda and Darcy as a couple, or that we are made acutely aware of the impossibility of a marriage between the early 21st and the early 19th centuries.

'A more gentle sensation towards the original': *pride and prejudice* as concealed autobiography

....

Revisiting the portrait of Darcy in Pemberley, Elizabeth develops a 'more gentle sensation towards the original' in much the way that the more we revisit the historical figure of Jane Austen, in spite of the surviving letters and the portrait of her by her sister Cassandra (in which she looks rather bad tempered), the more pleasing she becomes in both manners and looks. Like Shakespeare, given the little we know about Jane Austen, it is intriguing to see how so many readers and adapters have attempted to join the numbers and fill in the colours of the author's life. Since the very first adaptation, there has been a desire to read her novels as a means of finding out something about the author, a taboo up until recently in English studies, but a practice which is undeniably present in adaptations of Austen's work. In the television biopic, *Miss Austen Regrets* (2008), the attempt by Austen's niece Fanny to prevent her Aunt Cassandra from burning Jane's letters (as she notoriously did in real life) is met with the response: 'You still believe there is a secret love story to uncover?'[1] And as this very adaptation testifies, yes there still is a belief in an undisclosed love story.

The belief in a secret love story and the need to fill in the gaps of Austen's life, to create for her the romance she describes, is covertly present in the so-called 'straight' adaptations of Austen's fiction. *Miss Austen Regrets* is closest to *Persuasion* in its narrative, but while this Austen (played by Olivia Williams) is no saint, there has been a tendency to view the long suffering heroine of Austen's last novel, the repressed romantic, Anne Elliot, as a self-portrait of Austen herself, as in Anne Thackeray's comments of 1871, the year after the publication of the biography (or hagiography), the *Memoir of Jane Austen* by the author's nephew, James Edward Austen-Leigh: 'Anne Elliot must have been Jane Austen herself, speaking for the last time. There is something so true, so womanly, about her, that it is impossible not to love her. She is the bright-eyed heroine of the earlier novels, matured, chastened, cultivated, to whom fidelity has brought only greater depth and sweetness instead of bitterness and pain.'[2]

And if Anne is Jane at the end of her life according to Anne Thackeray, Elizabeth is implicitly identified as Jane as a young woman in film and television adaptations of *Pride and Prejudice*. As discussed in 'Cinematic adaptations of *Pride and Prejudice*, 1940, 2005', the connection between author and heroine is implied in both mainstream film adaptations of *Pride and Prejudice*. The similarities between Austen's refusal of Harris Biggs-Wither and Elizabeth's rejection of Collins are tempting to contemplate as is the 'final version' of Darcy and Austen's sketch to her niece Fanny of the perfect man:

[1] *Miss Austen Regrets*, directed by Jeremy Lovering, 2008.

[2] James Edward Austen-Leigh, 'Jane Austen', Cornhill Magazine, 1871, xxxiv. 158–74. Reprinted in Southam, vol. 2, p. 167.

There *are* such beings in the World perhaps, one in a Thousand, as the Creature You & I should think perfection, where Grace & Spirit are united to Worth, where the Manners are equal to the Heart & Understanding, but such a person may not come in your way, or if he does, he may not be the eldest son of a Man of Fortune, the Brother of your particular friend, & belonging to your own County. – Think of all this Fanny. Mr J.P. – has advantages which do not often meet in one person. His only fault indeed seems Modesty. If he were less modest, he would be more agreeable, speak louder & look Impudenter; – and is not it a fine Character, of which Modesty is the only defect?[3]

At the beginning of Robert Z. Leonard's 1940 adaptation, Elizabeth is positioned looking out of the window, framed by a wreath of lush flowers. The *mise en scène* serves to objectify her, framing her as a piece of art, positioning her for us to look at. In the latter half of the film, Elizabeth is frequently positioned looking out of the window, metaphorically being inside wishing to be out, with the spectator now looking with her rather than at her. Almost imperceptibly, the focus has changed and the viewer is now looking through Elizabeth's eyes, as if she has undertaken the position of omniscient narrator. The novel's famous first line is visualised in the opening sequence of this film when the women are shopping, at the moment when they catch their first glimpse of Bingley and Darcy, visually connecting shopping with courtship (referencing the novel's binary opposition between love and money and asso-ciating the ironic Elizabeth with the narrator). Joe Wright's 2005 film begins, in contrast, with Elizabeth looking inside the window, set apart from her family in the position of an outsider looking in.

[3] 'To Fanny Knight, Friday 18–Sunday 20 November 1814 Chawton' reprinted in *Pride and Prejudice*, ed. Gray, pp. 276–7.

However, by the end of the film, she's on the inside looking out, and as in the earlier film, she is implicitly likened to Rapunzel in her prison, waiting for her knight in shining armour to release her.

The 2005 film begins with a steadicam shot following Elizabeth up the garden path to Longbourn, enabling Elizabeth to lead us into her life, as if it is our own. She introduces the film by reading a novel, closing the book as she draws near her home, with a sigh of satisfaction having just reached its conclusion. The book's presence at the beginning of the film calls attention to the movie as an adaptation, nodding to the Disney technique of beginning a film with the opening of a book which metamorphoses into moving pictures, intimating that the moving images to come will be even more magical than the book it is based upon.

Close inspection (for those patient enough to capture the image on pause) reveals the book to be *Pride and Prejudice* itself, a witty acknowledgement of the film's source and status as an adaptation and a sly intimation that Elizabeth, like Austen, is in command of her own story and, possibly, an intertextual reference to *Bride and Prejudice* (2004) which used the same device, with Lalita reading the book on the beach with Darcy and Kiran (Caroline Bingley). While David Roche reads this meta-adaptive moment as an announcement of the film's infidelity to Austen, that the adaptation will leave the book behind to create something different, Elizabeth's possession of the book establishes a key connection between author and heroine.[4] The two film *Pride and Prejudice*s (1940 and 2005) invite connections to be drawn between Jane Austen and her central character, implicitly 'reading' the novel as

[4] David Roche, 'Books and Letters in Joe Wright's *Pride & Prejudice*: Anticipating the Spectator's Response through the Thematization of Film Adaptation', *Persuasions On-line*, 27 (2), 2007. http://www.jasna.org/persuasions/on-line/vol27no2/roche.htm. Accessed 09/05/10.

concealed autobiography. While the famous first line is absent from Joe Wright's 2005 film, Wright adopts other strategies of associating Elizabeth with her author. We're told on the special feature of the DVD that Elizabeth and Jane's relationship clearly echoes that of Jane and her sister, Cassandra. Whether this be true, the film does encourage us to replace Jane Austen's narrative voice, with Elizabeth's eyes (or the speaking 'I' with the seeing 'eye'), and the film is dominated by half face shots of Elizabeth's – or Kiera Knightley's — eyes, referencing Darcy's attraction to Elizabeth 'fine eyes' ('I have been meditating on the very great pleasure which a pair of fine eyes in the face of a pretty woman can bestow' (19)) while allowing the viewer to see things through these same eyes, that is Elizabeth's point of view.

The TV adaptations, likewise, encourage comparisons between Austen and Elizabeth with both the 1980 and 1995 adaptations giving versions of Jane Austen's famous opening line to Elizabeth. In 1980, the line is divided between Charlotte Lucas and Elizabeth, while in 1995 Elizabeth speaks it in response to her mother's premature scheming to marry Mr Bingley to one of her daughters. Elizabeth speaks the line, which could be attributed to Mrs Bennet, sharing the ironic perception of Austen's narrator in mockery of Mrs Bennet's ambitions, reinforced by the silly Mrs Bennet's nodding unwavering assent to Elizabeth's declaration. Associating the heroine of the story with Austen herself is not confined to *Pride and Prejudice*. Emma Thompson's Elinor in *Sense and Sensibility* (1996) and, more explicitly, Frances O'Connor's Fanny in *Mansfield Park* (1999) invite comparisons between author and heroine; however, it is Elizabeth alone who allows for a much more glamorous portrait of the artist as a young woman.

The implicit associations previously drawn between Elizabeth and Austen are nowhere more explicit than in the biopic of the author, *Becoming Jane* (directed by Julian Jarrold, 2007) which is almost a paint-by-numbers adaptation and biopic at the same time, perhaps a logical extension of previous adaptations' tendencies to unite the central character with the author, capitalising on what the press indentified as 'Austen Power'.[5] Biopics of authors are generally structured like a *bildungsroman*, a portrait of the artist as a young person, concentrating on the events leading up to success and ending with the price that success brings. The emphasis is on the dawning of authorship, the 'becoming' the person we know as the author.

The Romantic notion that art is inspired by love is strikingly central to films that depict the life of an author. While the Director's Commentary reveals unearthing early 1930s and 40s screwball comedies as models for the relationship depicted in *Becoming Jane*, other sources are clearly films that depict the life of an author or authors, such as *The Barretts of Wimpole Street* (1934) which sensationally recreates the love affair between the poets Robert Browning and Elizabeth Barrett. While normally despised by both film and literary critics for being both notoriously inaccurate and crudely formulaic, biopics continue to be a seemingly popular source of entertainment in the late 20th and early 21st century, given the list of titles, including *Iris* (2001, Iris Murdoch), *The Hours* (2002, Virginia Woolf), *Sylvia* (2003, Sylvia Plath), *Finding Neverland* (2004, J.M. Barrie), *Miss Potter* (Beatrix Potter, 2006) and *Bright Star* (John Keats, 2009). As Steve Neale explains, other common features include a conflict with a given community, prevalence of montage sequences, flashbacks, trial scenes, and/or a performance in

[5] See for instance, Jane Clifton, 'Austen Power', *The New Zealand Listener*, 27 January 2009, http://www.listener.co.nz/issue/3581/features/12473/austen_power. html. Accessed 26/03/10.

public.[6] *Becoming Jane* fits effortlessly into this template, the film beginning with Jane reading an excerpt of her work to a family party (after which she overhears the hero contemptuously dismissing it – 'Well, accomplished enough, perhaps, but a metropolitan mind may be less susceptible to extended juvenile self-regard' – echoing Darcy's famous overheard rebuke of Elizabeth in *Pride and Prejudice*) and ends with a mature Jane reading to an enthralled audience, including a now enraptured hero.

The adaptation formula, as described in 'A timeline of *Pride and Prejudice* adaptations',[7] is noticeably prominent in this film. In addition to endorsing hetero-normative values, adaptations that position themselves as adaptations, as epitomised by so-called 'straight' film and television adaptations of Austen's novels, contain recognisable features, including a fetishisation of history, music, words and books, a preponderance of intertitles, implicit or explicit tributes to the author, an emphasis on new media, references to art, either in or recreated by the *mise en scène*, and interpolations of female-friendly episodes. The emphasis on the period setting and music and an obsession with words and intertitles are stressed throughout. Jane's own writing introduces the film,[8] calling attention to her key characteristic and the nature of an adaptation that 'transforms' words into pictures. The foregrounding of 'new media' of the time is immediately presented to us in the opening credits with Jane's banging on the piano keys enacting both sexual and artistic frustration. Episodes in which Jane triumphs at cricket

[6] Steve Neale, *Genre and Hollywood* (London: Routledge, 2000), p. 60.

[7] See pp. 12–19.

[8] For a discussion of the intertitles, see Richard Burt 'Becoming Literary, Becoming Historical: the scale of female authorship in *Becoming Jane, Adaptation* 1 (1), 2008, pp. 58–62. Burt also observes a superficial resemblance to *Shakespeare in Love* but one, he argues, nothing like the copy-cat *Molière* (Laurent Tirard, 2006).

and in which Tom enjoys bouts of boxing, enabling the good-looking James McAvoy, like Colin Firth before him, to get out of his kit, explicitly cater for an adaptation's audience in which women are in the majority. *Becoming Jane*, like its predecessors, self-consciously creates familiar pictures, associated with the literary adaptation. Notable is the way that the *mise en scène* frames Jane, her sister, Cassandra, and her cousin, Eliza, in the corroding mirror in her bedroom, reminiscent of ageing portraits of female writers, such as the famously cracked pictures of the Brontës. Tom Lefroy (James McAvoy) is also framed in the style of Romantic portraiture, recalling in particular portraits of poets, such as the paintings of John Keats, Lord Byron, and Robert Southey, and as an object of the female gaze. The last we see of him as Jane's lover is a forlorn figure, framed by the carriage window, becoming smaller and increasingly insignificant as the carriage draws away. Ultimately he replaces Jane as the object of the film as this image revises an earlier one in which a rejected Jane is framed, almost identically, by the carriage window as she retreats from London, abandoning all hopes of a happy marriage.

Film 'readings' of Austen (probably) coincidentally mimic that of Austen's literary critical heritage, as discussed in 'The novel and its reputation', in which Austen becomes increasingly known as 'the prose Shakespeare' and second only to Shakespeare as literary genius.[9] It is undeniably the case that screen adaptations of Austen and scholarly work on Austen adaptations are second only to those of Shakespeare. And similarities between Shakespeare's most famous film biography, *Shakespeare in Love* (1998) and *Becoming Jane* (2007) have to be more than just coincidental. *Romeo and Juliet* and *Twelfth Night* are adapted in *Shakespeare in Love* by

---

[9] 'The novel and its reputation', pp. 26–27.

screenwriters Marc Norman and Tom Stoppard who rewrite the little we know about Shakespeare's life to reflect an author whose plays come from the heart, inspired by the personal experience of love. As Richard Burt argues, while critiquing mass culture, *Shakespeare in Love* depends 'on a very conventional way of representing literary authorship: Shakespeare's composition is privatized, and the sonnets and plays about love are granted a privileged generic status precisely because they are to be read as autobiographical documents'.[10] Ignoring the immediate source of *Romeo and Juliet* in Arthur Brooke's *Romeus and Juliet* (1562), this Will writes *Romeo and Juliet* as a direct experience of his forbidden love affair with a wealthy aristocrat, Viola De Lesseps (played by Gwyneth Paltrow) who is betrothed to and ultimately marries Lord Wessex (Colin Firth). *Becoming Jane*, similarly romanticises authorship by depicting 'real life' inspiration.

As in its forerunner, *Shakespeare in Love*, the author, with the perpetually inky fingers, gets many of her lines from those around her, including the first part of her most famous line from her thwarted suitor Mr Wisely (Laurence Fox), at the close of the film. Clearly, following from the success of *Shakespeare in Love*, Jane Austen, like Shakespeare, has now received the movie star makeover. Hollywood's need for an 'author' can be viewed in relation to the previous adaptations of the novel which often collapse the voice of the omniscient narrator into the character of Elizabeth Bennet. Indeed similarities between *Shakespeare in Love* and *Becoming Jane* are almost so obvious that the film risks the accusation of being dangerously derivative. Even the DVD covers

[10] Richard Burt, '*Shakespeare in Love* and the End of History', *Shakespeare, Film, Fin de Siècle*, ed. Mark Thornton Burnett and Ramona Wray (Houndmills: Palgrave, 2000), p. 216.

are remarkably alike, featuring embracing lovers filling most of the space, and a tiny picture of the author below them, visually suggesting a love triangle: an author caught between the love of her/his life and the demands of art. In the case of *Becoming Jane*, the lovers are literally separated by the pen in Jane's hand.

Not only replicating *Shakespeare in Love*, the film is also indebted to – or pays homage to – earlier adaptations of Austen's novels. Borrowing a number of costumes from the 2005 *Pride and Prejudice*, *Becoming Jane* visually recalls Joe Wright's movie, with Anne Hathaway's looks reminiscent of Kiera Knightley's Elizabeth.[11] The film 'rewrites' Jane as both Lizzie (in her initial repugnance for the man she eventually loves) and Lydia (in her decision to run away with Tom). The connections between Jane and Lydia are invoked and withdrawn (as Jane decides to abandon her lover so that he can embark upon a career, unhindered by her, to support his dependent siblings), but Jane's elopement, complete with red coat, recalls Lydia's costume in 1995 when she first sets eyes on Wickham. These red-coated women perhaps, on a subliminal level, recall Red Riding Hood, a visual signifier of the vulnerability of a woman on her own and an unconscious warning to the audience that the man she encounters is not all he seems to be.[12]

Typical of heritage adaptations, the film pays tribute to its own genre: the men stripping off and jumping into the lake references both *A Room with a View* and, of course, the 1995 BBC *Pride and Prejudice*'s famous leap in the pond. Jane's triumph at cricket echoes Greer Garson's Elizabeth's and Gwyneth Paltrow's Emma's victories at archery. The opening with the piano music, leading into Jane from behind playing the piano echoes the earlier film (where

[11] IMDB http://www.imdb.com/title/tt0416508/trivia. Accessed 28/04/2010.

[12] I am grateful to Natalie Hayton for suggesting this to me.

Mary is seen to be the musician, with her back to the camera): these opening shots bear an unmistakable similarity, with the piano player framed by a dark open door frame, drawing the viewer in to the warmth of the room. The farm animals, littered throughout this production, also recall the 'rustic' scenes in the Joe Wright adaptation of *Pride and Prejudice* (2005). There is a striking resemblance between Jane's cousin Eliza De Feuillide (played by Lucy Cohu) and Jennifer Ehle's Elizabeth of 1995 and a visual similarity between Wickham in the 2005 film (played by Rupert Friend) and Henry Austen (played by Joe Anderson) in *Becoming Jane*, especially in their tied back long golden hair. The *mise en scène* of Henry and Eliza's marriage echoes the marriage of Marianne and Colonel Brandon in Ang Lee's 1995 film, with the red-coated Henry and Eliza arm in arm descending the church stairs flanked by brightly coloured guests. In fact, this biopic is so immersed in its own generic associations that it becomes a curtain call of the most well-known Austen adaptations preceding it; on one hand, its dense and multi-layered intertextuality can be vigorously applauded, but on the other hand, it can be regarded as cynically cashing in on an over-worn commercially-driven formula.

Casting is another important feature in this adaptation that calls attention to its adaptation credentials in its recollection of earlier examples of the genre. While well-known actors bring their own particular spin to the parts, such as Julie Walters as Mrs Austen, and Lawrence Fox as Jane's thwarted suitor Mr Wisley, Maggie Smith as Lady Gresham is wheeled in as a toned-down Lady Catherine de Bourgh. Like Judi Dench in the 2005 adaptation, Smith's mere presence announces the film's credentials as a heritage production, bringing a host of other adaptation associations to the role, especially her roles as eccentric older woman in films such *Travels with My Aunt* (1972), *A Room with a View* (1985) *David Copperfield*

(1999) and, of course, Professor Minerva McGonagall in the Harry Potter films (2001–). The same case could be made for Ian Richardson, playing Tom's ill-tempered, patriarchal uncle, an actor renowned for character parts, including his role previous to this film as Lord Chancellor in *Bleak House* (2005). The choice of Anne Hathaway, an American actress, for the quintessentially English Jane, has its roots in the use of Gwyneth Paltrow as Emma (1996) or Renée Zellweger as Bridget Jones (2001), intimating that Austen and her characters belong to Anglo-American tradition rather than being exclusively British, perhaps as a gesture to flatter or placate the American audiences.

Becoming Jane is an adaptation of *Pride and Prejudice* insofar as it magnifies parallels between Jane Austen's life and the novel, originally entitled, *First Impressions*, begun in 1796, just before the film is set. As well as an adaptation of Austen's novel and numerous other film adaptations of Austen's work, the film is also an adaptation of Jon Spence's biography of the author, *Becoming Jane Austen*, in which Spence contends that *Pride and Prejudice* was inspired by the novelist's relationship with Tom Lefroy, the Irish nephew of Jane Austen's friend and neighbour – but while Jane is the reserved and proud Darcy figure, Lefroy, we are told, is more like Lizzie: he had five sisters to look after (and therefore couldn't afford an unconnected wife), his mother's maiden name was Gardiner (the surname of Elizabeth's aunt and uncle), and rather tenuously, the name 'Bennet' comes from Tom's favourite novel, *Tom Jones*.[13] For Spence, *Pride and Prejudice* is, on one level, a type of lovers' game, playfully littered with references to Tom and his family. Spence gives Jane Austen what she's successfully avoided for the last 200 years: a love life, indeed, he claims one so

[13] Jon Spence, *Becoming Jane Austen* (Hambledon: London and New York, 2003).

passionate that it sustained her for life and inspired her to write. According to Spence 'Tom Lefroy did not dwindle into insignificance: he found his natural place in her imagination, and remained there for the rest of her life'.[14] The romanticising of Austen's life is taken a stage further in the film which, for Lisa Hopkins, is in a mode 'reminiscent of nothing so much as the recent reissue of all Jane Austen's novels with chick-lit covers and the commissioning of a new "portrait" of her for Wordsworth Editions' "deluxe" edition of her works in which Austen is given "a bit of a makeover"'.[15] Like *Shakespeare in Love*, this film leaves no doubt about the author's sexuality, and ultimately the prospect that Jane can exist without a man is quickly dashed in the closing sequence, coming fast on the heels of the lovers' parting. The circulating shot, of the painted ceiling, adorned with putti, accompanied by the music of Mozart, momentarily plants the impression, in the audience's mind, that we are in Heaven. But no, Tom Lefroy's reappearance, several years after at a recital of an opera singer, completes the circle with Jane finally fulfilled in the knowledge that she is more than ever appreciated by the man she once loved. Rather than the author being celebrated for her work alone, the revelation of Tom's daughter's name, 'Jane', provides the film with its romantic climax.

This section has argued that the imposition of the biopic genre is a defining feature of literary adaptations – at least, adaptations of *Pride and Prejudice* – and it provides a structure that both centralises and de-centralises the author. *Becoming Jane* sits at the end of a long line of adaptations of *Pride and Prejudice* which collapse Jane Austen and Elizabeth Bennet, drawing heavily on its

[14] Ibid., p. 116
[15] Hopkins, p. 145.

credentials as an adaptation which simultaneously give and take away its sense of authenticity. In essence, theoretically, the valorisation of the author and the rigorous imposition of genre upon that life, that is the celebration of individuality through a well-worn formula, should not co-exist. André Bazin's observation that adaptations can only be valued and analysed once we cast off what is, after all, a very modern and possibly flawed idea of the author, when applied to the biopic, raises a number of problems.

> The ferocious defense of literary works is, to a certain extent, aesthetically justified; but we must also be aware that it rests on a rather recent, individualistic conception of the 'author' and of the 'work', a conception that was far from being ethically rigorous in the seventeenth century and that started to become legally defined only at the end of the eighteenth.[16]

Paradoxically, the biopic – in particular the film biography of an author - uses genre both to kill and resurrect the author. But, on another level, the biopic – and this is certainly true of *Becoming Jane* – exemplifies Bazin's point about authority in that ultimately the author is shown to be purely a work of fiction. This reading of the novel as veiled autobiography, doesn't seem to want to go away. Even in the 2008 TV mini-series, *Lost in Austen*, Elizabeth's absence is explained by the fact that she's away writing a book, a book which is inevitably, *Pride and Prejudice* itself.

[16] André Bazin, 'Adaptation, or the Cinema as Digest' in James Naremore, ed., *Film Adaptation* (New Brunswick, New Jersey: Rutgers University Press, 2000), p. 23

PART 3:

Critical responses and the afterlife of the novel's adaptations

'Heedless of the future': critical responses and the afterlife of the novel's adaptations

While the release of the 1940 adaptation generated relatively little press attention, by the 21st century an adaptation of a Jane Austen novel is a major event, almost always attended by the 'it can never be as good as the book' attitude. Fans of Austen adaptations, on the whole, cling to a need for fidelity to the text in spite of the fact that it is often the case that the most loved screen sequences are those that are added to the narrative; the most obvious example is Colin Firth's portrayal of an angst ridden Darcy and his famous emergence from a swim in the lake with his wet shirt clinging to his torso. Screenwriter Andrew Davies demonstrates, in this translation to screen, that the success of an adaptation is attributable to additions, or the filling in of narrative detail. Indeed this adaptation transformed Darcy from a stuffy and reluctant romantic hero into a full-blown Hollywood heart-throb, with an ever-increasing female fan base. This adaptation not only changed the popular view of the novel but also influenced later screen readings of *Pride and Prejudice*.

This book has endeavoured to answer the question: what is it that we learn from adaptations of *Pride and Prejudice* and why is there a seemingly insatiable cultural need for so many versions of the same story? Like Shakespeare, Austen is now an author who is regarded as a national treasure, and is a brand that signifies quality, tradition, culture, and stability. And when we think of an archetypal literary adaptation, Jane Austen or an Austen inspired adaptation invariably springs to mind. As argued in 'A timeline of *Pride and Prejudice* adaptations', pp. 3–24, the 'faithful' or 'straight' adaptation of *Pride and Prejudice* epitomises what qualifies as a 'classic adaptation'; it emphasises words, features works of art, period music, and pays tribute to the author. Also, the playing of the piano within the film is an instance in which the adaptation revels in itself as an adaptation, calling attention to its own form, a feature prophetically included in Austen's own novels in their depiction of the fascination and enjoyment of the new media, a pleasure recaptured in screen adaptations.

This book has observed how the most recent adaptations of *Pride and Prejudice* are, it would seem, as much dependent on previous film and television adaptations as they are on Austen's novel and rather than looking backward to an original text, point forward to future adaptations, based on the challenges each adaptation poses for its successor.

Following from Shakespeare, Austen on screen is now an established part of literary studies, as Pamela Church Gibson has demonstrated in 'Jane Austen on Screen – Overlapping Dialogues, Different Takes' (2009),[1] identifying edited collections as the mainstay of Austen on screen criticism, bringing together Austen scholars, political, social, cultural and garden historians, and film academics, especially those interested in heritage cinema. Laying the ground-

---

[1] Pamela Church Gibson, 'Jane Austen on Screen – Overlapping Dialogues, Different Takes', *Adaptation* (2) 2, 2009, pp. 180–90.

work for much of the material to follow is Sue Parrill's *Jane Austen on Film and Television: A Critical Study of the Adaptations* (2002), which includes detailed accounts of the numerous screen versions of Austen's works up until the beginning of the 21st century. Collections such as Linda Troost and Sayre Greenfield's *Jane Austen in Hollywood* (1998; 2nd edition 2001), Suzanne R. Pucci and James Thompson's *Jane Austen and Co.* (2003), Gina MacDonald and Andrew F. MacDonald's *Jane Austen on Screen* (2003), and David Monaghan, Ariane Hudelet and John Wiltshire's *The Cinematic Jane Austen: Essays on the Filmic Sensibility of the Novels* (2009) demonstrate that Austen on screen studies is catching up with Shakespeare on film as a major academic discipline. Lisa Hopkins has combined the two fields in her book, *Relocating Shakespeare and Austen on Screen* (2009), demonstrating how Shakespeare and Austen receive similar screen treatments. As in Shakespeare studies, it's now almost a requirement to mention screen adaptations in any book on the novels and, dutifully, the new *Companion to Jane Austen*, edited by Claudia Johnson and Clara Tuite (2009) includes an examination of Austen's reception and reinvention on screen. Unthinkable, in Austen studies up until the late 20th century, would be an entire issue of a respectable English journal devoted to a single film; it now seems totally reasonable that *Persuasions: The Jane Austen Journal On-Line* should choose to commit an entire issue (27 (2) 2007) to responses to Joe Wright's 2005 film of *Pride and Prejudice*.

The boom in the Austen on screen field was initiated, according to the editors of *Jane Austen in Hollywood*, in 'the United Kingdom in September 1995 with the "wet-T-shirt-Darcy" *Pride and Prejudice* mini-series'.[2] The apologetic, self-congratulatory superiority often felt by critics of Austen adaptations is articulated by Troost and

[2] Troost and Greenfield, p. 1.

Greenfield: 'On the one hand, we may wish the films good commercial fortunes as a way of seconding our appreciation, but on the other hand, this very confirmation of our taste renders our appreciation less exclusive, less a way of marking our superiority'. Essentially these volumes, while offering a variety of views and case studies, agree with Gina MacDonald and Andrew F. MacDonald's pronouncement that 'a good adaptation should take us back to the original work – what more could we ask from a couple of hours entertainment than to be reintroduced to past pleasures with a new perspective'.[3] Up until now, this seems to be the general ethos of Austen on screen studies, but it is slowly drifting away, with critics, such as Christine Geraghty, considering the screen versions in their own rights, without entering into unfavourable comparisons with the novels.[4]

This book began by arguing that *Pride and Prejudice* provides a template for one of the most popular of film adaptations: the romantic comedy. Innumerable examples of this genre can be cited, culminating in the lampooning of the formula in *Pride and Prejudice and Zombies*, 2009 (and soon to be a film, starring Natalie Portman, scheduled for 2011), a mixture of the 'real' novel with its most unlikely counterpart, horror fiction. This 'adaptation' of the novel has its origins in the 'mashups', web applications or pages that combine data from two or more sources, which can be found in abundance on YouTube. While it has been maintained that the novel's most well-known and uncontested adaptations seek to preserve Austen's novel in a pronounced emphasis on language and period detail, it's also undoubtedly the case that *Pride and Prejudice* can be detected in a myriad of other novels, films, and

---

[3] MacDonald and MacDonald, eds, p. 7.

[4] Geraghty, *Now a Major Motion Picture*.

television series in which the central couple lead split lives between what they say and what they feel, in variations on the battle between what Freud identifies as the ego and id. This conflict is neatly enacted in the classic rom-com, *You've Got Mail* (1998) in which the protagonists experience a virtual romance (through their e-mail correspondence) and a real battle over the survival of the heroine's beloved bookshop. The heroine, played by the queen of the genre, Meg Ryan, is, of course, a great lover of *Pride and Prejudice*, a cunning reminder to the viewer of the origin of the film's story, a film that also shares the novel's epistolary heritage, translating letters into e-mails. This is a rare confession in a rom-com and one that speaks for many in its covert message, going against the grain in current studies in adaptations which embrace intertextuality and the insignificance and impossibility of 'origins', by signalling a celebration of the literary in its homage to the film's author who is, at least in part, Jane Austen.

The novel's afterlife continues to extend itself and if we are to regard it as what Gérard Genette terms a 'hypotext' (even though it can be argued that it is itself an adaptation of previous stories), the proliferation and range of hypertexts is evidence of the work's undeniable canonical status. Genette's textual distinctions allow us to approach the offshoots of the novel from a variety of angles. For Genette in *Palimpsests: Literature in the Second Degree* (1982), a text can be regarded as a 'palimpsest', a work of art that is built upon a number of other artworks perceptible beneath the surface. While as Robert Stam notes, although Genette doesn't address film, his five subtypes of transtextuality ('all that sets the text in a relationship, whether obvious or concealed, with other texts')[5] are

---

[5] Gérard Genette, *Palimpsests: Literature in the Second Degree*, trans. Channa Newman and Claude Doubinsky (Nebraska: University of Nebraska Press, 1997), p. 1.

especially suggestive for the analysis of adaptation.[6] By modifying Genette's textual types to suit Austen adaptations, we can chart the novel's afterlife through the variety of forms it takes.

Intertextuality consists of quotations or allusions to other texts and develops from Julia Kristeva's notion of the concept of a literary work, consisting of intentional and unintentional references, quotations, allusions to and even plagiarisms of other works.[7] Genette considers this practice to be close to Harold Bloom's in *The Anxiety of Influence* (1973), in which the intertextual references are within the text (film) itself and, as in *Becoming Jane*, the jury is still out as to whether or not the numerous references to so many adaptations of Austen's novels can be regarded as a *tour de force* of postmodernity, building upon the 'charm of recollection', or an instance of a film that merely copies, steals and over-uses old devices. Adaptation as a 'collective memory' can be regarded as either innovative and exhilarating or stale, hackneyed, and clichéd.

Paratextuality refers to the materials surrounding the main text, and, for Genette, can take many forms, such as title pages, appendages, covers, typesetting, titles, genre indications, dedications, epigraphs, prehistory, intertitles, discursive texts, public responses, oral confidences and diaries.[8] Paratexts are commentaries and accessories that surround a text and in film adaptation these can include a dizzying range of materials, such as directors's commentaries, posters, reviews, music, toys, and other film tie-ins. As interpretative tools, paratexts can be both guiding as

[6] Stam and Raengo, p. 27.

[7] See Julia Kristeva, 'Word, Dialogue and Novel', trans. Alice Jardine, Thomas Gora, and Leon S. Roudiez, *The Kristeva Reader*, ed. Toril Moi (New York: Columbia University Press, 1986) pp. 34–61.

[8] Genette.

well as misguiding, the latter reminding us of the old saying: 'You can't judge a book by its cover'. A problem emerges, as almost always does in any system of classification, that there are intersections between these seemingly different types of texts, which blend into each other. It is possible to regard a film such as *Bridget Jones's Diary* as both hypertext (insofar as it adapts *Pride and Prejudice*) and paratext (insofar as it is a product of the novel). The paratexts of *Pride and Prejudice* can be found in a range of merchandising materials, for example the British Library sells replica note books, greeting cards and mugs embossed with the book's title. Websites devoted to Jane Austen, such as 'The Republic of Pemberley', 'Jane Austen's Tea Room' and 'The Jane Austen Fan Club' are themselves paratexts as well as including paratextual materials.[9] The most comprehensive of the websites is undoubtedly 'The Republic of Pemberley' and its welcome to newcomers anticipates a knowing reader, able to recognise the reference to Colin Firth's Darcy's request of his valet to bring him a special coat in which to greet Elizabeth at Pemberley (in the BBC 1995 adaptation):

Welcome to the Republic of Pemberley!

We, all of us, remember only too well the great relief we felt upon discovering this haven for Jane Austen Addicts. If your eyes did not widen, if you did not gasp in recognition, if you did not experience a frisson of excitement when you discovered a whole campful of soldiers – er – a whole websiteful of fellow Jane Austen Fanatics, then this place may not be for you. We are The

9 http://www.pemberley.com/
http://www.austen.com/phorum/list.php?4
http://www.fanpop.com/spots/jane-austen
Accessed 02/02/10.

Truly Obsessed here and have been known to talk for weeks about Jane Austen's spelling quirks and Mr Darcy's coat ('No, no – the green one.')[10]

On this ever-growing site is everything you could think of to do with Jane Austen, ranging from hypertexts, bibliographies, to bizarre lists such as the 'Jane Austen punishment list' which includes, 'An evening at a recital given by Mary Bennet, A tour of Rosings with Mr Collins or watching an episode of *Lifestyles of the Rich & Famous* guest-hosted by Mr Collins'. The site is a veritable treasure trove of everything to do with Jane Austen, including a list and reviews of over 50 sequels to the novel. It even features a shop selling water bottles, totes, a *Pride and Prejudice* game, filmographies, bibliographies, discussion boards and electronic editions of Austen's writings. 'Austen.com'[11] has a smaller array of Austen information and links with an additional feature allowing you to post your own Austen inspired story. 'The Jane Austen Fan Club' with over 1,500 fans offers another opportunity to share views on the novels, sequels and adaptations.[12] 'The Janeites'[13] is yet another site featuring information concerning Austen and Austen paraphernalia. In contrast to these is the Jane Austen Society whose aims are to preserve Austen's writing and foster the appreciation of her works and life. I could find no references here to adaptations of the novels.

Paratexts go on and on in almost every direction. The actors playing the roles become themselves paratextual as they invariably carry their before and after roles to the adaptation. Laurence

---

[10] http://www.pemberley.com/newbie.html. Accessed 02/02/10.

[11] http://www.austen.com/phorum/index.php. Accessed 07/02/10.

[12] http://www.fanpop.com/spots/jane-austen. Accessed 07/02/10.

[13] http://homepages.ihug.co.nz/~awoodley/janeites.html. Acessed 08/02/10.

Olivier's previous role as Heathcliff (1939) cannot help but affect the reception to his Darcy in 1940. Judi Dench (*Pride and Prejudice*, 2005) and Maggie Smith (*Becoming Jane*) bring previous associations to their parts, not least of which is their longstanding artistic respectability which can be seen to confront the young leading actresses who are implicitly invited to stand comparison. Anne Hathaway's confrontation with the grand dame of theatre and film, Maggie Smith, in *Becoming Jane*, invariably inspires comparison with her previous role in *The Devil Wears Prada* (2006) where she is head to head with America's leading lady of film, Meryl Streep. Kiera Knightley, inevitably brings to Elizabeth, Knightley's previous collection of roles, such as in *Doctor Zhivago* (2002), *Pirates of the Caribbean* (2003) and *Love Actually* (2003), and Elizabeth Bennet is somewhere behind her role as Cecilia in Joe Wright's later film, *Atonement* (2007), which begins with a similar steadicam shot of the main character, leading us into her life. Gemma Arterton's 'Bond Girl' in *Quantum of Solace* (2008) may bear traces of Elizabeth Bennet as much as Arterton's Elizabeth Bennet is a version of her character, 'Strawberry Fields'. Similarly it's possible to find traces of Kitty Bennet (*Pride and Prejudice*, 2005) in Carey Mulligan's Oscar award nominated performance as Jenny in *An Education* (2009) and, of course, Darcy embedded somewhere in Colin Firth's performance in *A Single Man* (2009).

Metatextuality is interpreted here as the commentary on a text within a text and in *Pride and Prejudice* adaptations, this often takes the form of self-consciously announcing the evolving set of generic features, as outlined in 'A timeline of *Pride and Prejudice* adaptations', pp. 3–24. Austen's own 'metatextual' comments on the alteration of the estate in *Mansfield Park* can be stretched here as a comment on the adaptation process itself that argues for only minor modification to what's gone before. Following from Alistair

Duckworth's *The Improvement of the Estate* (1971), Tim Watson considers Patricia Rozema's *Mansfield Park* (1999) in relation to the perception of improvement within the novel itself: 'Through the figure of improvement, then, the novel stages the difficult problems of how and when to change inherited social and cultural forms without thereby undermining their power to stabilise family and community structures: how, in other words, to manage and govern the effects of the past in the present, without risking sudden and potentially revolutionary innovation and change.'[14] Watson cites Fanny Price's uncharacteristically outspoken admiration of Mrs Grant's shrubbery: 'There is such a quiet simplicity in the plan of the walk! Not too much attempted.' She muses: 'perhaps, in another three years, we may be forgetting – almost forgetting what it was before.'[15] Taking the alterations to the estates, then, as an analogue for adaptation, if we could have Austen's own ideal formula we need look no further than Pemberley: 'where natural beauty had been so little counteracted by an awkward taste' (159). Allusions to the adaptation process, within the adaptation often serve to 'read', 'critique' or explain the alteration to source text itself. Examples of metatextuality are the references to the book itself, implicit in the 2005 adaptation of *Pride and Prejudice* while explicit in *Lost in Austen* (2009). In the novel and the adaptations, as we have indicated in 'A timeline of *Pride and Prejudice* adaptations', pp. 3–24, the playing of the pianoforte is another metatextual moment in which we witness an equivalent to the author's own artistic manipulation of the reader's enjoyment and emotion.

[14] Stam and Raengo, p. 57.

[15] Jane Austen, *Mansfield Park*, ed. James Kinsley (Oxford: Oxford University Press, 2003), p. 163.

Architextuality offers another take on the afterlife of the novel. Architextual materials include genre or the way a play, for instance, is structured into five acts. The title chosen is another architextual feature of a text. The range of names that *Pride and Prejudice* adaptations have taken is another dimension of the book's afterlife, posing questions about what distinguishes those films that retain Austen's title from those that don't. For example, what is the significance of changing the 'Pride', to 'Bride', in Gurinder Chadha's film adaptation?

Genette defines '**hypertextuality**' as a hypertext's relation to its hypotext and instances of this are approaches to Austen that reflect upon the adaptation's proximity to the novel, whether it be the attempted preservation of the language and context or the manner in which the adaptation translates thematic concerns into different media. The majority of work on Austen on screen has adopted this approach and it would be unfair to label it simply 'fidelity criticism' as often an adaptation can depart from its hypotext while at the same time offering new readings for a modern audience. This critical approach is at its worst when it merely applauds the adaptation for getting something right, adopting the self-consciously patronising *modus operandi*, identified by Troost and Greenfield that takes enormous pleasure in the belittlement of an adaptation in comparison to the novel, and is at its best when it demonstrates how the adaptation translates the words into different media, and makes us think of an old text in a new way; and as Genette writes, these can take many forms, among them parody, travesty, caricature and pastiche. An adaptation or a 'hypertext', like a palimpsest, a text that rewrites over an earlier one, expects itself to be overwritten by future adapters, allowing for varying degrees of the hypotext to be seen through its ever increasing layers. The variety of hypertexts have been interpreted for this book to consist of 'straight' television and film adaptations, adaptations that are loosely connected with the *Pride and Prejudice* narrative and adaptations that seek to read the story as, in part, the life of the author herself.

The afterlife of *Pride and Prejudice*, then, can be found in its ever-growing branches identified here as intertexts, paratexts, metatexts, hypertexts and architexts. The terrain of the paratext, in particular, points the novel in many directions, uniting with Austen in numerous capacities, from action figures, board games, mugs and stationery, and like the marriage of Wickham and Lydia, strangely compatible while still 'heedless of the future'.

selected further reading

Ailwood, Sarah 'What are men to rocks and mountains?': Romanticism in Joe Wright's *Pride & Prejudice, Persusions On-line*, 27 (2), 2007, http://www.jasna.org/persuasions/on-line/vol27no2/ailwood.htm. Accessed 10/05/10.

Aragay, Mireia, ed., *Books in Motion: Adaptation, Intertextuality, Authorship* (Amsterdam and New York: Rodopi, 2005).

Austen, Jane, *Pride and Prejudice* (London: Richard Bentley, 1833).

Austen, Jane, *Pride and Prejudice* (London: Blackie and Son Limited, 1894).

Austen, Jane, *Pride and Prejudice* (London: George Allen, 1894).

Austen, Jane, *Pride and Prejudice* (London: John Dicks, 1902).

Austen, Jane, *Pride and Prejudice*, ed. Donald Gray (1966 rpt. New York and London: Norton, 2001).

Austen, Jane, *Pride and Prejudice*, ed. Isobel Armstrong (Oxford: Oxford University Press, 1990).

Austen, Jane, *Pride and Prejudice*, ed. Pat Rogers (Cambridge: Cambridge University Press, 2006).

Austen, Jane, *Selected Letters*, ed. Vivien Jones (Oxford: Oxford University Press, 2004).

Barrell, John, *The Idea of Landscape and the Sense of Place, 1730–1840: An Approach to the Poetry of John Clare* (Cambridge: Cambridge University Press, 1972).

Bazin, André, 'Adaptation, or the Cinema as Digest' in *Film Adaptation*, James Naremore, ed. (New Brunswick, New Jersey: Rutgers University Press, 2000), pp. 19–27

Birtwistle, Sue, *The Making of Pride and Prejudice* (London: Penguin, 1996).

Bluestone, George, *Novels into Film: The Metamorphosis of Fiction into Cinema* (Berkley: University of California Press, 1957).

Boozer, Jack, ed., *Authorship in Film Adaptation* (Austin: University of Texas Press, 2008).

Brosh, Liora, *Screening Novel Women: Gender in the British Nineteenth Century Novel and its Film Adaptations* (London: Palgrave, 2007).

Burt, Richard, 'Becoming Literary, Becoming Historical: The Scale of Female Authorship in *Becoming Jane*, *Adaptation 1* (1), 2008, pp. 58–62.

Burt, Richard, 'Shakespeare in Love and the End of History', *Shakespeare, Film, Fin de Siècle*, ed. Mark Thornton Burnett and Ramona Wray (Houndmills: Palgrave, 2000), pp. 180–203.

Butler, Marilyn, *Jane Austen and the War of Ideas* (Oxford: Clarendon Press, 1975).

Cardwell, Sarah, *Adaptation Revisited: Television and the Classic Novel* (Manchester: Manchester University Press, 2002).

Cardwell, Sarah, *Andrew Davies* (Manchester: Manchester University Press, 2005).

Carroll, Rachel, ed. *Adaptation in Contemporary Culture: Textual Infidelities* (London: Continuum, 2009).

Cartmell, Deborah and Imelda Whelehan, eds, *Adaptations: From Text to Screen, Screen to Text* (London: Routledge, 1999).

Cartmell, Deborah and I.Q. Hunter, Heidi Kaye and Imelda Whelehan, eds, *Classics in Fiction and Film* (London: Pluto, 2000).

Cartmell, Deborah and Imelda Whelehan, eds, *The Cambridge*

Companion to Literature on Screen (Cambridge: Cambridge University Press, 2007).

Cartmell, Deborah and Imelda Whelehan, *Screen Adaptation: Impure Cinema* (Houndmills: Palgrave, 2010).

Cavell, Stanley, *Pursuits of Happiness: The Hollywood Comedy of Remarriage* (Cambridge Mass: Harvard University Press, 1981).

Crusie, Jennifer, ed. *Flirting with Pride & Prejudice* (Dallas: Benbella Books, 2005).

Doyle, Carol M., 'Jane Austen and Mud: *Pride & Prejudice* (2005), British Realism and the Heritage Film', *Persuasions On-line*, 27 (2), 2007, p.5/10, http://www.jasna.org/persuasions/on-line/vol27no2/dole.htm. Accessed 8/05/10.

Duckworth, Alistair M., *The Improvement of the Estate: A Study of Jane Austen's Novels* (Baltimore and London: Johns Hopkins Press, 1971).

Eckstut, Arielle, *Pride and Promiscuity: The Lost Sex Scenes of Jane Austen* (Edinburgh: Canongate, 2004).

Elliott, Kamilla, *Rethinking the Novel/Film Debate* (Cambridge: Cambridge University Press, 2003).

Fielding, Helen, *Bridget Jones's Diary* (London: Picador, 1997).

Fielding, Helen, *Bridget Jones: The Edge of Reason* (London: Picador, 1999).

Foster, Jennifer, 'Austenmania, EQ, and the End of the Millennium', *Topic: A Journal of the Liberal Arts* 48 (1997): pp. 56–64.

Fowler, Karen, *The Jane Austen Book Club* (London, New York, Toronto: Penguin, 2004).

Genette, Gérard, *Palimpsests: Literature in the Second Degree*, trans. Channa Newman and Claude Doubinsky (Nebraska: University of Nebraska Press, 1997).

Geraghty, Christine, 'Foregrounding Media in *Atonement*', *Adaptation* 2 (2), 2009, pp. 91–109.

Geraghty, Christine, *Now A Major Major Motion Picture: Film Adaptations of Literature and Drama* (Lanham, Boulder, New York, Toronto, Plymouth: Rowman & Littlefield, 2008).

Gibson, Pamela Church, 'Jane Austen on Screen – Overlapping Dialogues, Different Takes', *Adaptation* 2 (2), 2009, pp. 180–190.

Giddings, Robert and Erica Sheen, eds, *The Classic Novel from Page to Screen* (Manchester: Manchester University Press, 2000).

Greenblatt, Stephen, *Shakespearean Negotiations: The Circulation of Social Energy in Renaissance England* (Oxford: Clarendon Press, 1988).

Hamilton, Paul, *Historicism* (1996; 2nd ed. London: Routledge, 2003).

Hannon, Patrice, 'Austen Novels and Austen Films: Incompatible Worlds?' *Persuasions* 18 (1996): 24–32.

Harding, D.W., 'Regulated Hatred: An Aspect of the Work of Jane Austen', *Scrutiny* 8 (March 1940), 346–62.

Harman, Claire, *Jane's Fame: How Jane Austen Conquered the World* (Chatham: Canongate Books, 2009).

Higson, Andrew, *English Cinema, English Heritage: Costume Drama Since 1980* (Oxford: Oxford University Press, 2003).

Hopkins, Lisa, *Relocating Shakespeare and Austen on Screen* (Palgrave: Basingstoke, 2009).

Hutcheon, Linda, *A Theory of Adaptation* (New York and London: Routledge, 2006).

Jerome, Helen, *Pride and Prejudice: Dramatized from Jane Austen's Novel* (Garden City, NY: Doubleday, 1936).

Johnson, Claudia L. and Clara Tuite, eds, *A Companion to Jane Austen* (Oxford: Wiley Blackwell, 2009).

Jones, Darryl, *Critical Issues: Jane Austen* (Houndmills: Palgrave, 2004).

Kaplan, Laurie, 'Lost in Austen and Generation-Y Janeites', *Persuasions On-line*, 30 (2), 2010, http://www.jasna.org/persuasions/printed/pers30.html.

Kennedy, Margaret, *The Mechanized Muse* (London: George Allen & Unwin, 1942).

Leitch, Thomas, 'Adaptation Studies at a Crossroads', *Adaptation* 1 (1), 2008, 63–77.

Leitch, Thomas, 'Adaptation, the Genre', *Adaptation*, 1 (2), 2008, 106–120.

Leitch, Thomas, *Adaptation and its Discontents* (Baltimore: Johns Hopkins University Press, 2007).

Looser, Devoney, ed., *Jane Austen and the Discourses of Feminism* (New York: St Martin's Press, 1995).

Lynch, Deidre, ed., *Janeites: Austen's Disciples and Devotees* (Princeton and Oxford: Princeton University Press, 2000).

MacDonald, Gina and Andrew MacDonald, eds, *Jane Austen on Screen* (Cambridge: Cambridge University Press, 2003).

McFarlane, Brian, *Novel to Film: An Introduction to the Theory of Adaptation* (Oxford: Oxford University Press, 1996).

Monaghan, David, Ariane Hudelet and John Wiltshire, *The Cinematic Jane Austen: Essays on the Filmic Sensibility of the Novels* (Jefferson: Mcfarland, 2009).

Neale, Steve, *Genre and Hollywood* (London: Routledge, 2000).

Parrill, Sue, *Jane Austen on Film and Television: A Critical Study of the Adaptations* (Jefferson: McFarland, 2002).

Poovey, Mary, *The Proper Lady and the Woman Writer: Ideology as Style in the Works of Mary Wollstonecraft, Mary Shelley, and Jane Austen* (Chicago: University of Chicago Press, 1984).

Pucci, Suzanne R. and James Thompson, eds, *Jane Austen & Co: Remaking the Past in Contemporary Culture* (New York: State University of New York Press, 2003).

Roche, David, 'Books and Letters in Joe Wright's *Pride & Prejudice*: Anticipating the Spectator's Response through the Thematization of Film Adaptation', *Persuasions On-line*, 27 (2), 2007.

http://www.jasna.org/persuasions/on-line/vol27no2/roche.htm.

Sanders, Julie, *Adaptation and Appropriation* (Abingdon: Routledge, 2006).

Seeber, Barbara K., 'A Bennet Utopia: Adapting the Father in *Pride and Prejudice*', *Persuasions On-line*, 27 (2), 2007, http://www.jasna.org/persuasions/on-line/vol27no2/seeber.htm.

Southam, B.C., ed., Jane Austen, *Volume 1 1811–1870: The Critical Heritage* (1979; rpt. Abingdon: Routledge, 2009).

Southam, B.C., ed., *Jane Austen, Volume 2 1870–1940: The Critical Heritage* (1987; rpt. Abingdon: Routledge, 2009).

Spence, Jon, *Becoming Jane Austen* (Hambledon: London and New York, 2003).

Stam, Robert and Alessandra Raengo, eds, *A Companion to Literature and Film* (Oxford: Blackwell, 2004).

Stam, Robert and Alessandra Raengo, eds, *Literature and Film: A Guide to the Theory and Practice of Film Adaptation* (Oxford: Blackwell, 2005).

Stam, Robert, *Literature Through Film: Realism, Magic, and the Art of Adaptation* (Oxford: Blackwell, 2005).

Sutherland, Kathryn, *Jane Austen's Textual Lives: From Aeschylus to Bollywood* (Oxford: Oxford University Press, 2005).

Tanner, Tony, *Jane Austen* (London: Macmillan, 1986).

Todd, Janet, ed., *Jane Austen in Context* (Cambridge: Cambridge University Press, 2007).

Troost, Linda and Sayre Greenfield, *Jane Austen in Hollywood* (1998; 2nd ed. Kentucky: University of Kentucky Press, 2001).

Turan, Kenneth, 'Interview with Ann Rutherford (Lydia), Marsha Hunt (Mary) and Karen Morley (Charlotte Lucas)', *Persuasions*, 11 (1989), 143–50. http://www.jasna.org/persuasions/printed/number 11/turan2.htm.

Turan, Kenneth, '*Pride and Prejudice*: An Informal History of the

Garson-Olivier Motion Picture', *Persuasions*, 11 (1989), 140–43, http://www.jasna.org/persuasions/printed/number11/turan.htm.

Wagner, Geoffrey, *The Novel and the Cinema* (Rutherford, NewJersey: Fairleigh Dickinson University Press, 1989).

Webster, Emma Campbell, *Lost in Austen: Choose Your Own Jane Austen Adventure* (New York: Riverhead Books, 2007).

Whelehan, Imelda, *Helen Fielding's* 'Bridget Jones's Diary' (New York: Continuum, 2002).

Wilson, Cheryl A. '*Bride and Prejudice*: A Bollywood Comedy of Manners', *Literature/Film Quarterly*, 34 (4), pp. 323–332.

Wiltshire, John, *Jane Austen: Introductions and Interventions* (Basingstoke: Palgrave, 2006).

Wiltshire, John, *Recreating Jane Austen* (Cambridge: Cambridge University Press, 2001).

index